DATE DUE

JE 26 '97			

DEMCO 38-296

Storming the Desert

A Marine Lieutenant's Day-by-Day Chronicle of the Persian Gulf War

by

SEAN T. COUGHLIN

McFarland & Company, Inc., Publishers
Jefferson, North Carolina, and London

The names of military personnel below the rank of colonel have been changed to preserve the privacy of those individuals.

British Library Cataloguing-in-Publication data are available

Library of Congress Cataloguing-in-Publication Data

Coughlin, Sean T., 1965–
    Storming the desert : a marine lieutenant's day-by-day chronicle
of the Persian Gulf War / by Sean T. Coughlin.
        p.   cm.
    Includes index.
    ISBN 0-7864-0195-8 (sewn softcover : 55# alk. paper) ∞
    1. Persian Gulf War, 1991— Personal narratives, American.
2. Coughlin, Sean T., 1965–   .   I. Title.
DS79.74.C695   1996
956.704'4245 — dc20
    [B]   96-27287
                                                                                CIP

Manufactured in the United States of America

McFarland & Company, Inc., Publishers
    Box 611, Jefferson, North Carolina 28640

Table of Contents

Preface

In June 1990, Saddam Hussein invaded Kuwait, and in December that same year, like so many other U.S. service people, I deployed to the Gulf expecting the worst. We all expected numerous casualties, but it quickly became apparent, to me at least, that Saddam Hussein had no idea what he was doing, was a terrible military leader, and in no way warranted the fear we held for him. The unusually short war over, we returned home disgusted, more ashamed than proud, hailed as heroes. It seemed a lot to get used to as we mourned the fallen few, especially those who died in Dahran, but get used to it we did as we went on with our lives.

Storming the Desert is a day-by-day account of the war written from a second lieutenant's point of view. I think you will find evidence of the fear that we all felt, along with the eventual disgust, and really come to know what it was like in the trenches during the war. Little has changed with time, and I think it is apparent in the text where myopia got the better of me in what I was reporting. I tried to maintain my objectivity, but I kept the subjective side of my writing unchanged to give you a better overall impression of just what it was like to experience at first hand the conflict now known as the Gulf War.

My training was as a logistics officer, and I worked in this position for Marine Wing Support Squadron (MWS) 37, in support of the Third Marine Air Wing. Like all Marine officers, I attended the Basic School for my initial training and then went on to Little Creek for my subsequent schooling in logistics. I was then stationed with Marine Wing Support Squadron (MWSS) 372 at Camp Pendleton, California, where among other things I served as the Maintenance Management and Rear Area Security Officer. When war broke out, I was sent as an augmentee to MWS-37, the parent command to MWSS-372, and I worked as a Special Staff Officer with that unit throughout the Persian Gulf War. Thus I was in a privileged position before, during, and after the war to see a great deal of what goes on in the Marine Corps during a campaign, and *Storming the Desert* is an immediate reflection of those observations.

I have tried to be honest and tell it as it was. When I was writing in my journal, I felt I had no superiors to answer to and no punches that I had to pull, so the journal is as honest an account as there could be of the Gulf War. As a lieutenant, I was in a position to see and do a great deal more than others did. I was on the road a great deal, taking care of support group business, and I think my observations will speak for themselves.

The Gulf War was a tremendous experience for me, probably the defining moment in my life. Going off to war expecting the worst and living through all that we did was probably the biggest thing that I'll ever experience. There are still prayers to be said for those who died, but our cost in casualties was little short of miraculous in terms of the number of people involved, and for that I'll be forever thankful. So please read *Storming the Desert* in the spirit that it is presented — in as honest a tone as possible and in the expectation that we can always work to better ourselves and our performance as soldiers. If *Storming the Desert* achieves this at all, it will have met its purpose.

Sean Coughlin
Los Angeles, California
Spring 1996

Chapter 1

December

15 December 1990 (Saturday)

We're sitting around Norton Air Force Base watching Staff Sergeant Emerson, Staff Sergeant James, and a few other guys playing bones, waiting for the plane to arrive which will take us to Saudi Arabia. They're jiving and joking with each other in a pleasant sort of way, and I start thinking back on how fast everything's happened to get me here.

On Monday there was a frost call for an additional augmentee to the group staff. Everybody was already sick of being told that our squadron was going, only to find out time and again that it wasn't. And I myself was tired of getting my hopes up of going as an augmentee with another squadron, only to find others filling those billets ahead of me. So it was with bitter frustration that I heard on Monday that the Group staff needed another junior officer. I no longer wanted to go because I had accepted the fact that I wouldn't get the chance to and convinced myself that that was the way it would be. The only reason I did add my name to the list of volunteers was the fact that as a Marine I felt I could do no less.

So the next morning, on Tuesday, as I slipped into the outer office of the headquarters building to read the message board, I was shocked to hear the XO giving my name to Group over the phone as the MWSS-372 nominee for the billet. I was stunned and felt a sudden surge of anger. This wasn't what I was prepared for; I already had other plans. Maybe an article for the *Gazette* and more time to train for the 1992 Olympic Team. These were the projects that I had planned to work on during the course of Operation Desert Shield to keep my mind off the fact that I wasn't going, and here everything was changed in the space of a few minutes.

It still wasn't definite that I was going. My name had only been submitted as the MWSS-372 nominee, and surely the other support squadrons would

1

be sending in their nominations as well, but the billet called for a lieutenant who could write, and I started feeling that this time was for real. But anyway, I thought, they would be sure to tell me if I was going, so I went back to work and didn't think much more about it.

That night I told my wife that there was another chance I might be going. Like all the other wives in the squadron, she'd heard this a dozen times before, so she just laughed and made a joke about it, expecting it to be like every other time, that I'd come home the next night and tell her that we were not, in fact, going, and that I'd be safe at home with her throughout whatever was going to happen.

The next day I went in and asked the XO what was up.

"So am I going, sir?"

"Hell, yes, and you better start packing, you're leaving Friday."

A thrill of fear, delight, and anger. Why the hell hadn't he told me yesterday? I had about four days to turn over the Maintenance Management Office and the armory, to get fitness reports done on all my Marines, to take care of some administrative and legal matters I had pending at the command, and to give my wife, Maryanne, the best Christmas I could before leaving. Instantly my life went into overdrive.

I went back to my office, sat around for a few minutes, then organized and wrote down everything I had to do, and went to it. Turning over the MMO was easy. The lieutenant who took it over was an LDO maintenance officer and probably knew the job better than I did. Next came the armory. I turned it over to my boss, the squadron logistics officer, and then said goodbye to all of my armorers. All of them had done great work for me and I'd truly miss them.

That night at dinner I was quiet.

Maryanne asked me, "Well, are you going?" fully expecting the answer to be no and being ready to tease me for giving her a false alarm yet again.

I smiled at her, bittersweetly I thought, and said yes.

For a moment she was stunned, then she broke down and cried. I held her close and did my best to calm her down, but I didn't know what to do or say that would make her feel any better.

Wednesday I got up early and went in to work to turn over the last of my projects. I cleaned out my desk, finished up the last few administrative duties I had to take care of, and said goodbye to my clerks. They were the first troops I'd had in the Marine Corps, and we'd been through a lot together. Finally, I said goodbye to my friends, who all wished me good luck, and went off home.

I still had a lot of shopping to do, and that was the next thing to get done. I bought everything I was told to bring and whatever I thought I'd need. Extra socks, green T-shirts, laundry bags, laundry clips, insect repellent, shoe laces, captain's and lieutenant's bars (I'd been selected captain in April of 1990 and if, as expected, we'd be over there for over a year, or if there were heavy casualties, I'd most likely pin them on, or so I thought), soap, razors, shampoo, etc.

The lady at the exchange was great and used her own list to make sure I had everything I needed.

Then I had to go back and get my 782 gear from the MWSS-372 Supply Section. Two sets of NBC equipment, canteens, H-harness, helmet, flak jacket, long underwear — again, everything that was required or necessary.

Finally, I checked out my weapon and K-bar from the armory. That night I just relaxed with my wife, and went over again and again the last few things I'd need to round out my kit.

A bunch of us had gone to desert survival school a few months earlier, and I spent Thursday putting together my survival kit. I went from one outdoor shop to another, from drugstore to drugstore, picking up odds and ends of survival tools that would be invaluable in any survival situation but would fit into a small bag. Rubber tubing to get at water in fissures, cracks, and wells. A space blanket, matches, candles, a razor blade, parachute chord, a Swiss army knife, plastic bags to carry water; getting all this stuff took forever. When I was finally done, I'd had enough of shopping and just went home to get all this stuff ready.

Once packed I relaxed a bit, then ran off again to finish the last of the tasks on my list. That night would be Christmas, and I wanted to make it as special as I could for Maryanne. I bought her a pair of gold and silver earrings and some yellow roses. That night we bought our tree at Target, and we celebrated our first Christmas together early. She held back her tears, and I took pictures for her to send me when she got them developed.

I called my parents and told them I was going. My father said to be careful and to make sure I took care of my men. My mother cried, and I did my best to calm her down. She just said to be careful and that she loved me and that she thought everything would be all right. My brother Kerry said good luck, and my brother Ryan, at TBS, said he was jealous and that he wished he was going as well.

More friends called. More people crying over me and making me feel special. It was such a wonderful feeling, all this love and affection. Then Maryanne opened her presents, and I opened mine. She had given me some books to take with me and some sketch books in which I could begin drawing. I had always intended to learn how to draw, and she gave me everything I needed to start. I felt bad about this stuff at first because I wanted to travel light and the books would be a lot to carry, but I knew I'd have to take them because they just meant too much, coming from her, to leave behind.

The next day was Friday. That night I'd be leaving. I spent the day with Maryanne. For a few hours I went boogie boarding in the ocean — who knew when I'd see water again? At the end of it, I felt good, cold and tired.

Early that night Maryanne made me a spinach pasta dinner. I said one last goodbye to my parents, brothers, and friends. Laura, a close friend of ours from college, almost cried when I told her I was leaving. I never knew how sad and touching all this could be. It was like a dream. Maryanne and I lay on the couch and watched "Rudolph the Red-Nosed Reindeer." Both of us were quiet and emotionally exhausted, and I was so happy just to lie there and watch "Rudolph," which I'd loved as a child, with my beautiful wife on a chilly December night.

We dozed. Finally it was time to go. I loaded up with as much gear as I could carry, while Maryanne took the rest. She was wearing clothes I'd given her for her birthday in October and some things she'd bought on our honeymoon in September. As we went down to the car, I thought of how strange it was to be leaving in the middle of the night like this. I wondered what the other people in the apartment complex would be thinking if they looked out of their windows and saw this Marine leaving in the middle of the night packed to the gills with equipment and gear. It was so quiet, and everything was wet from an evening shower.

The rest of the night was a blur. Kissing Maryanne goodbye. The buses loading and taking off from the barracks. Colonel Mitchell and the other guys saluting us. The wives waving goodbye. And me happy, smiling, but sad. I was really going to war. Although I know war is terrible, it's what I'd secretly always wanted to do. Tolstoy was right, there's no escaping it. Man is invariably drawn to it, seems pathologically fascinated by it.

I was sitting next to Sergeant Kofu, a giant Samoan Marine, who was already asleep as I settled back into the seat. It was a tight fit and uncomfortable. I was tired, but couldn't sleep. Two hours later we were at Norton Air Force Base.

At Norton we unloaded the buses and packed our gear against the side of the building. Then we went inside to wait. I met Lieutenant Potter, the officer whose billet I was filling, and right off she told me how bummed she was that she couldn't go. She said she had some medical problem that precluded her deploying, but that in time she'd find some way to get over there. I also bumped into Katie Kerrigan, another lieutenant and fellow Naval Academy graduate. She was an intelligence officer and filled me in on what was going on over there. Her feeling was that Tarik Aziz would find some way to avert a war and that this buildup was all a show of force and of our intention to back up the UN resolutions.

I sat down to wait, thinking about how unreal this all felt. It seemed strange to think that I might actually get killed over there and that Maryanne's life would go on without me in it. I thought of all the lives my death would touch, my parents, my friends, and how quickly your life could be snuffed out. I had always thought that if I did go off to war, I'd just not think about making it home alive, I'd just accept the fact that at some time in the course of the war I'd be killed. I thought that would make me fight better — almost as if I had nothing to lose. Of course all this thinking was just the result of the time we had on our hands and of the suddenness of the deployment; I just didn't really know what to expect.

16 December 1990 (midair)

We got off from Norton around 1830. I had called Maryanne about 1200, before we left, and she sounded pretty good. In the air we were treated like royalty by the stewards and stewardesses. They kept bringing us loads of food, cookies, snacks, and drinks. I love cookies and I ate a ton of them. It almost felt as if they were fattening us up for the kill. What do they know that we don't? We slept all the time. Because I'm an officer I got to fly first class with the rest of the officers and SNCOs. I kinda felt guilty about this, but it was one of those times I let rank have its privileges. One MP lieutenant, Lisa Dean, sat in back with her troops. But since I had none to worry about, I didn't really sweat it. I sat with Joe Espinoza, another Academy grad, class of '89, brand new from logistics school, who was going to MWSS-373 in the billet I thought I'd be getting about a week ago. He's a good guy and a good friend, and the flight just flew by with us joking about how easy this all is and how crazy it was back at 372 jumping through the hoops all the time.

The flight engineer was a former Marine and kept waking us up with his terrible jokes and ooh-rah speeches.

"What happens when you have nine odds and ends on a shelf and you take away eight? What's left, an odd or an end?"

"De plane! No, de boat! De car! Besides, we're in de plane."

We landed in New York about 1130 and left around 0100, headed for Brussels, Belgium. On the way across the Atlantic, we watched Madonna videos and *Days of Thunder*, which is not the greatest of movies.

At 1920, Belgium time, we took off from Brussels.

17 December 1990

I lost all sense of time or day on the flights. We'd gained eleven hours since leaving California — three going to New York, five or six to Brussels, and two or three to Bahrain. At about 0400 in the morning, we arrived in Bahrain.

Finally, Arabia. I was excited as hell. I'd always dreamed of going to Arabia, after studying Islam and the Arabs in school, and I could hardly wait to get a breath of the air. I wanted to smell it, to see if I could sense the land's holiness. This was the land of Allah, of Islam, and of a truly devout people. While we waited on the runway, we said goodbye to all those Marines who were debarking in Bahrain. A lot of them were from 372 because most of them were augmentees from the Wing going to MWSS-373. I said goodbye to Joe and told everyone God bless and good luck.

They filed down the staircase and into the early morning darkness. They formed up, read roll call, grabbed their baggage, and went off into the dawn, just as the sun was rising. I stood on the top of the staircase and watched them go. I was hoping I'd see the sunrise, but just as the sun was breaking over the horizon we had to pile back into the plane and strap in. The last leg of our trip would be north to Jubail.

It seemed as if we'd been on the plane forever, although it was a very comfortable and restful trip. The flight attendants all said goodbye, one even broke down over the intercom and said "God bless you all."

It sent goose bumps down my spine. I guess people are really behind us on this one.

18 December 1990

I think. We waited at the airport for a while, long enough for me to eat a frankfurter MRE, until our baggage showed up and the buses to take us to the soccer stadium where we'd be staying. Of course I was the only one who ate. I'm always hungry and just chow down the MREs like there's no tomorrow, until I get sick of them, which is pretty quick.

Chief Warrant Officer John Clark and I are the only two from MWSS-372 who've been assigned to the Group staff, so we kind of stick together. He was an MP in Vietnam, he knows how to take care of himself, and he's a nice guy. He's also kind of taken it upon himself to look out for me. Somehow he got a ride for us with Major Stevenson, the S-3A, who came over with the advance party.

We climbed in one of the civilian trucks and took off for King Abdul Aziz Naval Base, where the soccer stadium is located in which we'll be living. On the way I was spellbound by the fact that I was cruising around in Saudi Arabia. I'm here, I made it. The airport was pretty desolate and sandy, as we'd expected, but the lands around the highway leading down to King Abdul Aziz are like nothing I would have expected. They're just like regular roads, and there are oases all over the place. Jubail is actually quite a populated and livable place.

It's strange how you come to expect the land and people of places you've studied to be the same as the way you imagined them to be years ago. You don't expect them to be industrialized or modern or very similar to your own country, but they are. I expected the Arabia of Abdul Aziz ibn Saud and Abdullah bin Jaluwi. I found a modern, fully developed, twentieth-century country. I was a bit disappointed, but at least could imagine what it must have been like only decades earlier, when this land was locked away from the rest of the modern world. In a sense I was even unhappy that we're here, because it means that these holiest of holy lands are being defiled by men and armies who have no appreciation or sense of the history that lies beneath their feet.

At about 0700 we arrived at the soccer stadium. It was a complete surprise and totally different from anything I'd expected. I had prepared for the worst, expecting to be living far out in the desert, away from any creature comforts or conveniences. I had even brought one pair of civilian clothes that could double as military garb in a bad situation. The soccer stadium seemed more like a hotel than a tactical encampment.

Right off, John hitched me along, and we went off to check out the place. There were showers in the stadium itself, an exchange, a hamburger stand, and GP tents, built right on top of the pavement. The entire stadium parking lot was covered with tents.

I thought the whole thing had bad news written all over it. I saw no perimeter, no reaction force, no central command post. The planes were lined up end to end on the airfield, and there were only two small guard posts where they checked incoming vehicles for the proper identification. I just prayed that a commando force wouldn't have the balls to attack us.

I'm also depressed about the fact that I just seem to be a small cog in this monstrous machine, and I have so little effect on anything that happens. Our duties aren't clear yet, and as with any new job, it's easy to get disoriented and depressed. You always imagine that you'll be doing wonderful and important things, making important decisions, and making a difference. Then reality sets in, and you realize you're just a very small, maybe insignificant part of something that is so much larger than you ever imagined.

19 December 1990

Today I just watched everybody setting up our headquarters and office spaces. We'll be working out of three separate trailers. One for the CO, XO, sergeant major, and S-1; one for the S-2 and S-4; and one for S-3. Our headquarters and service squadron will be working out of hardback tents, as will the armory and supply people. The Group is Marine Wing Support Group 37, out of El Toro Air Base in California. Its mission is to provide all essential ground support requirements to the Air Wing.

We do this by coordinating the efforts of the Marine Wing Support Squadrons that are directly beneath us in the chain of command. The Support Squadrons are stationed at each Marine air base and provide such things as fuel, engineering support, and expeditionary airfield services. The MWSSs provide anything that the planes need to keep flying outside of avionics and aviation logistical support. When a plane comes in leaking fuel or ready to burst into flame, it's the MWSSs who provide the fire trucks and crash fire rescue teams. When they have to lay matting to add on more runway for the planes, it's the MWSSs who provide and lay the matting. All the fuel, food, and anything else on the ground side that the pilots, flight crews, and air support people need to keep going is provided by the MWSSs. Our job is to coordinate their activities and assist them as well as we can.

I'm depressed, as usual, and thinking about the SEALs and Marine Corps infantry, wishing I was with them instead of here. Yesterday we unloaded a few of the embark boxes Group 37 worked so hard to bring over here. They were full of frisbees, softballs, all kinds of games, and baseball visors. The coffee pot seemed to be the most important thing of all and definitely got the most attention. I guess I'll just have to wait until I start working to feel good about myself again. I owe Maryanne a letter, at least I can get that taken care of today.

John knows I'm in the dumps and is always telling me to relax and just see how things go. He's already found us nails, wood, and a bunch of other stuff that he's stashed in our tent for future use. He's definitely made it easier to fit in here. Christmas is coming up soon, too.

A bit later we were sent off to Bahrain, where our parent command, the Third Marine Air Wing, is located, to get copies of all the reports we're supposed to submit to them. I saw Joe Espinoza again, Chris Bowden, a friend from TBS and logistics school, and James Wentworth, whom I rowed with at the Naval Academy. I had become very close to him when we traveled from Little Creek, Virginia, to Annapolis, Maryland, every weekend to see our girlfriends, now our wives, when we were at logistics school. I also met the 373 MMO, Terry Avery.

John and I had all our gear on, canteens, first-aid pouch, gas mask, pistol and magazines, and our survival kits, which I had so painstakingly assembled, and of course right off Chris and Terry laughed uproariously, telling me that in a few weeks the only things I'd still be wearing were my gas mask and pistol, which were required at all times.

Everybody looked good. James looked even bigger than I'd remembered him. He had that lean, hard, serious, down-in-the-dog look that comes with long, hard work. He had been there since August, working every day without a day off. We talked about what we saw as a general lack of planning on the support side — not having enough alternators, needing to contract out to the civilian community so much, little things that were missing like wood for bunkers and concertina wire, and basically the trouble the CSSDs were having supporting people.

Word is that it's still going to be some time before we're ready to fight.

20 December 1990

Today I climbed the lights around the stadium and made a rough sketch of the area we live in.

Rick Dezelic took me up there. He's the construction officer at MWSS-174, the unit that supports the King Abdul Aziz Air Field. I met him while he and his guys were pouring the concrete for the pads between our headquarter's trailers. At first I was disgusted that we'd be pouring concrete between the trailers, just to make the place more comfortable, until somebody explained to me that doing so was practical as well. It would keep dust and dirt out of the offices and would protect our computers.

This sounded good, but we still have no bunkers, and Rick told me they still need to pour concrete down at the Avionic work areas, and that their

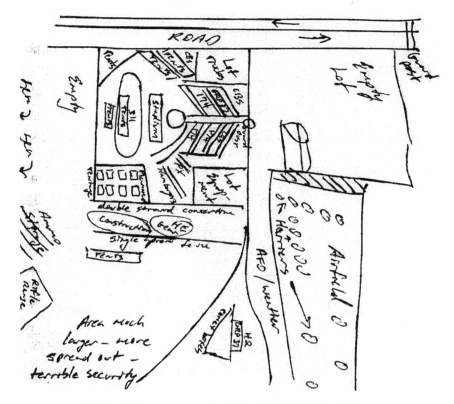

Sketch of the encampment at King Abdul Aziz Naval Base.

equipment particularly needs to be kept clean and working. Rick also told me that he was supposed to be putting in a barbecue pit soon.

Naturally, Rick isn't too happy about all this either. We became fast friends, and when I told him I'd love to be able to get the layout of the place he had me follow him toward the stadium and then up the tower. It was a great view, with the whole camp, airfield, and naval base spread out below us.

We're short of wood, which is why the bunkers are taking so long. I guess it doesn't matter anyway, though, because the CO of the MAG in charge of the airbase told Rick to knock off work on the bunkers since "we're now on the offensive and don't need them anymore."

21 December 1990

Today we had a scud alert. I heard it come in over Jerry Barron's radio, "incoming scud — this is not a drill." At first we thought it wasn't happening.

It couldn't be for real. Then, slowly, we all began moving, still not actually believing it was for real, but feeling that we'd better do something.

John and I started hustling everyone out of the offices and outside and sent them running toward another unit's area, where we'd heard there were bunkers, since we had none of our own. I ran through the offices one more time, checking to make sure they were empty. I stopped in one to drop off a message I'd been carrying and then ran outside myself.

Outside I saw two Marines a few yards away going about their business on a forklift. Still no alarms had sounded at the stadium, and there was no sign that anything was amiss. It was strange knowing everybody else was running for the bunkers while these two guys were working on the forklift, as they would on any other regular day, with obviously no clue of what was going on around them.

I ran up and told them, calmly, that I thought this was all kind of weird and not a little like a joke, but that there was a good chance we had scuds inbound and that they'd better get the hell out of there.

They didn't waste any time. They shut down the forklift and took off while I ran back toward where the others had gone.

I was alone. Then I heard somebody yell, "three minutes to impact," and for the first time it hit home and I really started running. I can't believe it, I thought, he really did it. Goddamn, he really did it.

I imagined the missiles cruising through the sky, like something out of a cold war picture, where the missiles are launched and they can't recall them. I wondered if I'd see them break the horizon and come cruising in toward the stadium. I wondered if there'd be people hit, or if we could just get low and let them explode above us.

I found the trench, jumped in, and started running down it. Time to get the gas mask out. I came to a bunker — full. I ran to the next one. It was only a hole off the side of the trench, but I thought it looked good enough. I only hoped the trench itself would be deep enough for us to lie down in for protection.

There were about four other Marines there. One didn't have a hood to his gas mask and was waiting outside the bunker with his weapon drawn and at the ready. I put on my gas mask and couldn't breath. "Relax," I told myself, "relax," but I still couldn't breath. "I must be hyperventilating," I thought. "You got to relax!" I tilted the mask up, then lowered it again. Still couldn't breath, maybe this is what those guys felt like in World War I.

Not really, my air filter was stuck and wouldn't allow me to exhale. That was the only problem, and it was my own fault because I should have checked it. I exhaled hard once and opened the filter — the mask worked.

I kept waiting for the harriers to take off, but nothing happened. Then finally we heard the "all clear."

Everybody was pretty shaken up. Now we all have a sense of what's going on and the seriousness of the whole situation. Even the powers that be. All of a sudden bunkers have become a high priority.

We're short on sandbags, engineer stakes, and concertina wire, but have plenty of games, letters, frisbees, coffee, extra food, you name it. We're still short on alternators. There's also still a wood shortage, but everybody in the camp has tons of furniture, shelves, bookcases, chairs, beds, tables, and walls made of wood.

MWSS-174 does have a rear area security detachment, but the perimeter is way out, unmanned, with no interlocking fields of fire that we're aware of.

Televisions and VCRs have appeared. Last night we had an Air Force band playing in the Scud Bowl. John almost died when he saw a few Air Force girls dancing and singing backup. I just hope the time doesn't come when we have to pay the piper.

For minimal security measures, we at least need sirens, NBC gear, reaction drills, and holes. "Take charge, make things happen, Lieutenant." Sometimes it just seems as if you can't get anything done.

22 December 1990

Saw a bigger picture today, or at least a glimpse of it. Saw the Group commander and squadron COs planning for the emplacement of their units. So many considerations — food, fuel, ammo, construction, etc.

Other considerations: movement, emplacement, logistic needs, convoys, showers, food, refrigeration units, vat cans, billeting, wood, tents, fuel, water, overflow contingencies (especially at an air base), acquisition and security. Amazing how much goes into all this. Still, I can't help but think that there's a definite lack of concern with the rear area security problem.

Have to always remember to think like the Romans did, who set up a fully fortified defensive position every night on the march. It was just a natural part of how they operated as a military force, and though it was probably a real pain building a regular fort every night, it shows how important security measures were to them. They were second nature.

Imagine if the Marines did this as well, thinking of security as a natural and inherent part of everything we did. If we thought that way, throughout the ranks and in every branch of the Marine Corps, we'd be invincible as a fighting force. Who the hell would want to fight an outfit like that?

23 December 1990

Today we worked on message traffic, trying to establish MWSG-37 as the parent command of the MWSSs, who are now so used to operating on their own and reporting directly to their respective MAGs and the 3D MAW that they really don't want to report to us. So we're getting message traffic established between them, us, and the Wing, to ensure that it flows the way it should. Naturally the Colonel wants this to have happened yesterday.

I also began looking for things to do that would make me more useful around here. I still don't feel as if I have a job yet, and it doesn't look as if things will be changing anytime soon in that regard. We just kind of saunter into work, do a few odd jobs, like getting messages out, close up and head off to chow, and then bed. Not a real exciting life.

So I've decided to set myself up as a kind of operator. I'll find out what the squadrons need, like alternators, find out how to open purchase it out in town or where I can trade for it with stuff I can get more easily and set myself up as a key source of supply. A problem solver.

I went to Jubail Port and Jubail Airport today with Captain O'Brien and Lance Corporal Kutchner, and wherever I go I make a point of finding out what the maintenance sections are short of. That's the first step, finding out what people need.

The ride over there was fun. Captain O'Brien is a nice guy and has a lot of the same interests I do. He's an NFO who was mistakenly sent to flight school after finishing the Infantry Officer's Course and getting assigned to a battalion at Camp Lejeune, North Carolina. We talked forever about how hard it was to get the bunkers in, and how easy it was to do anything else.

Anyway, the trip got me out of the doldrums. A change of pace, different scenery. I guess the office was just getting on my nerves. Nothing to do there, just sit, read, write, and wait. Out there you could relax. And the good conversation just added to it. Good conversation is the spice of life; it makes you feel alive and glad to be living.

The guards at Jubail Airport were the best I've seen yet. They had double check points, and at the main check point they made you open your hood and they checked underneath the body of the vehicle with a mirror on a carriage. At King Abdul Aziz, there is still no sentry at the second check point, and maybe two at the first. There were about four at Jubail Airport.

We saw "Good Morning, Vietnam" tonight at the "Suds and Scuds" bar. They only serve nonalcoholic beer and soda, but it is the only place we have to go and hang out. They have darts there, places to sit down and relax, and television, with movies every night. Captain O'Brien said he'd met a pile of English nurses there on Saturday, and I was hoping they'd be there again, but no such luck. Just guys, bummed and thinking of home.

It's weird how involved in movies you can get. They're like a drug, taking you completely away from this place, or any place, getting you so involved in what's happening in the movie that you forget all sense of yourself. Then when it's over you almost feel better because you've been revived in a way. Things don't seem so serious; after all, watching "Good Morning, Vietnam" in Saudi Arabia is just like watching it at home.

Our tent is beginning to feel more and more homey. It's pretty much of a mess, but most of that is from Jerry Healey and Tony Rominger, who've laid claim to one entire end. I'm trying to steal *The Big Sky* from John to read, and for some reason tonight he and English started talking about Kat in *All Quiet on the Western Front* and about another book called *Johnny Got His Gun*. I think John's getting sick of hearing me talk about being up front with the grunts. "Be happy where you are," he says, "that's where God put ya."

25 December 1990

Merry Christmas! I got through to Maryanne on the phone tonight, which is hard to do, but she wasn't home, and all I could do was leave a message on the answering machine. At least I got to say Merry Christmas to her; there are many people over here who won't be able to do that. Boy, do I miss her.

Last night, Christmas Eve, we had a little celebration in the tent. Tony told stories of his drill instructor days at the recruit depot in San Diego—what a wild man. It's hard to believe he's the same guy that's bummed out because he misses his wife and kids and the same guy that'll take you under his wing and take care of you. Now he's a warrant officer, like John. Must be something about those guys, always looking out for the new kids.

We ate the last of the little orange candies Maryanne had sent with me, a few bags of chips, and had some cokes. Not a bad little celebration.

Today we had a real Marine Corps feast. The food services guys really knocked themselves out, and it was pretty good. Turkey, ham, jelly, you name it, somehow they brought it all in.

Before dinner we had to go to the airport again, so Captain O'Brien could get something squared away with the Seabees. On the way back, we stopped in at the British Army Hospital to find the English nurses that Captain O'Brien was so eager to get in touch with. Since that night at the "Suds and Scuds" I'd heard of nothing else. Too bad for O'Brien, he didn't find any there. All we got out of that little sojourn was a box of mincemeat pies, which a Scotsman gave us as a Christmas present.

Going to bed this night thinking of my wife and how lucky I am to have her. I was so terrified of getting married, of losing my individuality, and thinking back on that and what I put her through, I can't believe I didn't lose her. Thank God for that.

26 December 1990

I went down to Bahrain again today. John Clark and I went to visit 373 and get some MPS issues straightened out. The main thing we had to do was make sure they understood how they'd be getting their gear from Jubail Port down to Bahrain after it was unloaded from the MPS ships. Would they send operators and drivers up to grab the stuff as it came off? Or would they wait until the equipment was staged and then send drivers up to bring it back?

MPS stands for Maritime Pre-positioned Shipping. The idea is to have the newest and best equipment prestaged on merchant vessels throughout the world so you can move the ships quickly to wherever they're needed, unload them, and have the equipment, gear, and supplies necessary to fight a prolonged, heavy engagement. So far things seemed to have gone off fairly well. We're pretty much ready to go with all the MPS gear, which must be some kind of rapid deployment first, although I have heard there were a few problems.

One thing that did not go off so well with the MPS ships was the offload and distribution of equipment. People are calling it the "Maritime Pre-positioned Steal" and are saying you rated whatever you got away with. Supposedly, infantry units were taking heavy engineer equipment, aircraft maintenance men were walking off with tanker helmets, and just about everybody was stealing HUMMVs. I'm even hearing stories of colonels and majors telling lance corporals to get off equipment they were driving and then making off with it.

The big thing with all this appropriation going on was to make sure that 373 had people at the port when the gear came off, even if they wanted it staged. That way, we hoped, we'd prevent it from getting stolen.

While we were down there, I saw James, Chris, Terry, Joe Espinoza, and a bunch of other people that I knew. As usual we solved all the logistic and security problems of the Marine Corps that afternoon, and, as usual, I probably said more than I should have about what I thought. Later when I was with the S-3 from 373 I told him how Colonel Caldwell had divided up the gear among the squadrons. He did it by sitting down with a pencil and doing it himself. I told the major that I didn't understand why the squadrons didn't sit down with him and work it out that way. They were all mad at each other, each thinking the other was stealing all the equipment, or getting more that its fair share, and maybe one squadron could trade something they didn't really need all that bad for something they did.

Afterwards John took me aside and told me I better quit shooting my mouth off. That you never say anything that could reflect negatively on your boss in front of others. Naturally I felt pretty bad about this; sometimes I just don't know when to shut up.

On the way back we rode over the causeway, smelling the sea air and watching the sun set on the Gulf. Bahrain always smells so much like home, summer, and fresh sunny days.

30 December 1990

It's getting harder to keep up with the journal. Missed a few days there. Since Wednesday I've spent a lot of time on drawing, work, and letters. Today's been slow. Working on reports, the asphalt road for 374, and B-rations for 373. Yesterday I worked on a letter of instruction for Rapid Runway Repair and a bunch of situation reports. Most of the stuff I do is easy to take care of, and I spend most of my time just sitting around, reading, and writing.

My plan for becoming "Mr. Parts" has kind of gone out the window. Now I'll do my best to get the stuff if I have the opportunity, but I won't be able to set myself up as an operator in the way I wanted to. To buy parts out in town you need to have Blanket Purchase Agreement authority. I don't have this and I can't get it, so my plan's finished before I even got it off the ground.

The phone system is all bunged up. We can call home, but we can't call 174 three hundred yards down the street.

I also found out that the Seabees have 60MM mortars. It's part of their thinking, but obviously not part of ours. We have no idea how we even fit into the airfield defensive plan. And it's no better at the airfield in Bahrain. James told me the ammunition supply point down there has only eleven men guarding it at any one time. If something were to happen to it, either an accident or intentional sabotage, the place would blow up an area with a seven mile radius from ground zero. Reminds me of *A Raid on Rommel*.

Everything is "Hoss" now. Because of *The Big Sky*, John and I have started calling each other Hoss. We call everybody else that, too, but a few people don't like it. I guess for now we'll just keep it to each other.

"Hoss" is Gunner Clark, Chief Warrant Officer 4 Clark. Served with the Army M.P.s in Vietnam, broken time, came back in with the Marines. Looks like an old man, heavy, tired, excitable. "I'm too old for this shit." For me he makes this place bearable. I'm always listening to his tales, laughing with him, and teasing him for going to bed so early. He falls asleep almost every night at seven. After he reads about fifteen minutes, the book just plops down across his face and he's asleep.

Snores all night and curses when he has to get up in the middle of it to take a piss. The Seabees built a pissing tube out back among the bunkers. Almost every night you wake up and gotta take a leak. It seems cold as hell now, I never thought it would get this cold here, and it's a real pain in the ass to climb out of bed, get your shoes on, shuffle out there, then find the right trajectory to hit the funnel for the tube without getting it all over you. I don't know if our bodies just haven't got used to the time change yet or what.

Also in our tent are Lieutenant Jerry Healey, Warrant Officer Tony Rominger, Captain George "English" O'Brien, Warrant Officer Richard Perry, Major Howard, and sometimes Lieutenant Dan White.

Healey's an LDO. An engineer by trade, he works in the S-3 as the plans officer. What he mainly does, like everybody else, is do what Colonel Caldwell needs done. He's a good guy, and I've already learned enough from him about maintenance since I've been here to be a dangerous man when I get back to 372. It's easy to see why Colonel Caldwell depends on him so much because he gets things done. He can be cruel, and strange in a peculiar way, but he's an easy guy to get along with.

Rominger's the former drill instructor. A real hard Marine. He's small, about 5'6" or so, but he carries himself like a big man, and a tough one. He's not a guy you'd want to have as an enemy. He's also a real hard worker and gets things done. He works as the group embark officer in the S-4. He was a grunt for seventeen years, but to stay in he had to move into embark. He hates it, though he works hard at it, and he's always telling me stories of being in the infantry. Sometimes I think he's even going to take off and join one of the units he knows up there. We'll wake up and he'll be gone. I've been sticking close to him, because if he does go, I'm going with him.

Tony and I both grew up in Massachusetts. We're very different — he's from Boston, I'm from the Cape — but we get along well. I can't wait to go home; I don't think he's been back since he left seventeen years ago. He told me he joined to go to Vietnam and just missed it. Now he's sitting out this war down here.

George "English" O'Brien. Redheaded, pale-skinned, soft, and definitely out there. The easiest way to describe English is harmless. I get along well with him, but he really doesn't do a whole hell of a lot. Constantly late for work. Oversleeps every day. Always seems to be in some kind of pain or discomfort: bad back, bad legs, you name it. English is in habitually dire straits. He does not do anything for work either. I don't think he knows what it means to get things done. He keeps waiting around for people to tell him what to do, and when they do he does such a half-assed job of it that it's usually a waste of time anyway.

There's not a lot of work to be done in the S-3 anyway since Colonel Caldwell does almost everything himself, but when he does have you do something he usually needs it done quickly, and he needs it done right.

Colonel Caldwell is right out of the movies. He's a good old boy from Arkansas who came up through the ranks, first as an enlisted guy, then an LDO, and finally an officer. As a lieutenant colonel, he's reached as high as the Marine Corps will let him go without having come in with a regular commission. He seems as if he's been in the Marine Corps forever, which is practically the case since he went through boot camp almost ten years before many of us were even born. There's very little he doesn't know about getting things done in the Marine Corps, and he usually just sits back calmly and lets it all happen while everybody else is running around yelling about all the things that need to get taken care of.

He's also loyal as hell. You work well for him and he'll take care of you. I can kind of sense this with Jerry. Right now I'm on a trial basis. Colonel Caldwell can be awfully exasperating, though, because he never lets us know what the hell is going on, which is especially hard since I'm supposed to be writing up the significant events every day, but he's definitely growing on me. He's also levelheaded as hell and never seems to get worked up about anything, which is a good way to be if you're in the kind of position he is. I ought to follow his example more often; I'm always getting worked up about everything.

You can tell Colonel Caldwell has just given up on English. He's useless to him, so he just doesn't depend on him for anything. He ignores him. English's problem is that he doesn't realize that you make ground slowly, that you just have to do each job the best you can until people start depending on you and going to you to get things done. It's easy to think that there's a pattern to working in the Marine Corps, or anywhere for that matter, but there isn't. You can do as little, or as much, as you please.

English hangs around, reads, tells stories, and then teaches karate to some of the troops in the early evening just before dinner. I was going to start going out there, but John told me not to. "You stay away from him." Funny, even with his karate, I think English was pretty helpless. He grew up in Hawaii, and I think he must have had a pretty miserable childhood. He was a "howie," or white kid, and at the end of the Hawaiian school year they have "howie" day when the Hawaiian kids beat up on all the white kids.

He's still fun to be with, though, because he talks endlessly about the Arabs, British soldiers, and the Foreign Legion. He smokes this ridiculous pipe, sings these weird ass English ballads just before he goes to bed, and wears his hat backwards, so he can peak it in front. I think he fancies himself an English adventurer, a throwback to an earlier and more romantic time of empire.

Perry's another guy who's definitely out there. I try to argue with him every now and then, but half the time I don't know what the hell he's talking about. He makes his statements as if they were the last word on any particular subject we are discussing and then moves on to explain the next topic on which he's expert. He usually comes in at night, literally shuffles around for minutes at a time, crinkles something up, starts eating, shuffles around some more, then climbs into bed and goes to sleep. Whatever this strange routine signifies is a complete mystery, but he does it every night.

Perry's slight but wiry and usually looks as if he's just not quite getting what you're talking about. He served in Vietnam, with "Force." This may be true, but if every guy who says he served with Force Reconnaissance in Vietnam, or in any of the Special Forces for that matter, actually did so we would have had the biggest SEAL, Green Beret, and Force Reconnaissance force in history. I guess nobody served in the support establishment over there. Everybody was in the bush, even though it takes about seven support people to put one fighting soldier in the field for almost any conflict. With Richard, though, you have to believe him, for whatever reason.

Major Howard sleeps across the tent from John and me. He rates a CP tent because of his rank, but he stays with us instead. He's the Group S-4. A supply officer by trade, he took over the 4-shop when Major Hardy, the old S-4, moved to MAG-11. He's very approachable and is always talking my ear off about logistics and everything else. He's also a Southern boy, born and bred. He said his grandmother wouldn't allow a Yankee to step foot in her house as long as she lived. I guess that's why the joke I made about Sherman flying through Georgia didn't go over too well with him. That's when I realized how serious he was about this stuff.

He also loves busting on Academy grads, or graduates of the "prick factory" as he calls it, but he's always the first guy to go to for information or help if you have any kind of a problem, professional or otherwise, and he usually knows the answer you need or at least where to find it. Colonel Coop and Lieutenant Colonel Caldwell both swear by him, and he is a hell of a supply officer.

The Major's kind of the mediator for the tent. Tony, Richard, and Dan White all work for him, and since they're usually the ones at each other's throats, he spends a lot of time in the tent making sure that things don't get too out of control. He's also an invaluable source of information. If it wasn't for him, none of us would have the slightest idea of what was going on. He makes a point of briefing us every night, filling us in on what's up with the Group and how it all fits in with the big picture.

Dan White, the Group supply officer, sleeps next to me, but he's rarely here and seems more like a ghost than anything else. He usually sleeps down at the headquarters and only shows up to shower or grab some of his gear.

And as usual, Hoss is snoring away, dreaming of his cute little Mexican girls.

31 December 1990

I'm experimenting with my leadership style. I'm trying to be a hard ass with Gunney Hendrix to see if it works better than the way I usually am, which is quiet and low key. Force is not one of my strong points.

What I'm finding is that being a dick isn't really getting me anywhere with him. They always tell you to be natural and to lead the way you feel most comfortable with and believe gets the best results. So I think it's about time I went back to what's tried and true for me. I'll do what I always do, be quiet, lay low, find out the lay of the land, work myself into the system, then go for it. You accomplish more that way than you ever do if you try to push too hard too fast.

Last night we had another scud alarm. I was really relaxed and cool, taking charge, leading them into the bunker, and then making sure that everyone was calm and prepared for whatever happened while we waited there. I just wonder if I'd be that way in a real attack, after the missiles had hit. At least I'm doing okay so far.

Later that night I thought I heard three gunshots and then some shouting. At TBS you'd be in a half sleep waiting for the attack to come, and when you could hear the shots and the faint yelling you knew it had. I guess in the back of my mind I expected the same thing to happen here because I thought our biggest threat would be terrorists or commandos infiltrating into the camp. I jumped up, shouted "John" as I clawed through the zipper of my sleeping bag and was just pulling my pistol, which I slept with beside me, when Lieutenant Colonel Staunton, the Group XO, came in. I pointed the pistol straight at him.

"Put that pistol down!" he ordered.

I earned my call sign out of that little adventure. At TBS they called me the Quantico Fox, and at 372 they called me Mad Dog. At MWSG-37, I became Quick Draw, and Hoss became Babaloo.

*   *   *

In December, MWSG-37 deployed to Southwest Asia in support of Operation Desert Shield. At that time MWSG-37 took over operational and administrative control of all the MWSSs in country, which included MWSS-174, 271, 273, 373, and 374, and it established itself as the 3D MAW command and control element for all aviation ground support requirements.

MWSG-37 set up reporting procedures, accounted for all equipment and material within the squadrons, and prepared for the emplacement of MWSS-271 and 273 as they arrived in country. Engineer and support equipment continued to arrive from CONUS by both sea and air and was redistributed accordingly.

By the end of December, MWSG-37 was fully operational and gainfully employed fulfilling all of 3D MAW's aviation ground requirements. Engineering, refueling, motor transport, expeditionary airfield, billeting, food, and communication were just a few of the services that MWSG-37 provided in support of the air effort for Operation Desert Storm.

Chapter 2
January

Worked on the bunker today and yesterday. It's good, hard labor, and it's making me feel better about myself and my job. I can kind of come and go as I please and work on whatever needs to be done. Today there was nothing pressing administratively in the S-3 shop, so I went out back with the working parties and started filling and stacking sand bags.

The bunkers are built out of wood at the MWSS-174 construction shop and then transported to the places where they'll be set in by the heavy equipment operators. At the designated positions, they have a bulldozer or backhoe dig out a hole in the ground, and this is where the bunker goes. Because the ground we're on is so close to sea level and the water table is so high, the bunkers are only buried about three to five feet in the ground and the rest of the structure sticks up above it.

This is not what you want to have in a good covering position. You want to get as deep as you can, with as much dirt over your head and around you as possible. To make up for this problem, we fill sand bags and stack them around the bunkers. The idea of the bunkers isn't to protect you from a direct hit, or even a hit in the general area, but from shrapnel and flying debris. I think. Sometimes I'm not sure anybody knows what the purpose of the bunkers is, that is just what they told us, or what the general consensus is.

The bunkers themselves are built out of beams of thick, heavy wood, which is what we seem to be forever short of. Understandably, of course, since trees don't really grow that well in the desert, but frustrating, nevertheless, when you see the attention and foresight we have shown with everything else that has been brought over, like carpets and office furniture. So bunker construction proceeds at a pace of fits and starts, based on the availability of wood and whenever it comes in.

The Group headquarters has three bunkers emplaced around it now, and working parties are called up from all the different sections to fill in the areas around the bunkers, to fill up sand bags, and to stack them around and over the bunkers themselves. I have fun doing it, probably because I don't have to do it all the time. The rest of the guys, mostly staff sergeants, sergeants, corporals, lance corporals, and privates, are already sick of it. John has come out a lot as well and is forever saying he can't believe that he is doing this again. That he must have filled "thousands of these fuckers" in Vietnam.

And, as always, "I'm getting too old for this shit."

It does scare him, and I see it especially with him filling the sand bags. I guess it brings back bad memories. And with the threat of gas, which he didn't have to deal with in Vietnam, things are doubly worse. John just doesn't know what he will have to deal with, which is hard for an older man.

They say war is a young man's game, and now I know why. The older guys just take it too hard. It wears them out. They worry. The younger guys don't know what to expect, but most of them don't care. Emotionally, it's a hundred times harder on the older guys, which means physically everything else they do breaks them down that much more. You have to be in good shape to handle this, and for whatever reason, most of the older guys aren't.

Work is going along smoothly. I'm reading Richard Henry Dana's *Two Years Before the Mast* and working on my drawing, so I can show Maryanne the progress I made in the sketchbooks she gave me when I get home. Dan Quayle was here yesterday, and I was bummed that I missed him, but I didn't want to knock off work on the bunkers. One of the guys who works as a clerk and driver in the S-3, Corporal Hall, is from Indiana and went to see him talk at the stadium.

Today Robin Williams is doing "Good Morning, Saudi Arabia" for us on the radio, and everybody has been tuned in all day. Out on the bunkers I did my best to listen, but all I had to hear it on was this tiny hand radio that one of the troops brought out which I could hardly hear. Almost everybody else had a Walkman, which were given out by the USO to the younger troops, and worked in silence, laughing out loud at the jokes, which those of us without radios couldn't hear.

Earlier tonight in the tent Tony and I were messing around with our pistols and making Hoss nervous. He is nervous as hell around all these "wackos with weapons," as he calls us, so we go out of our way to get him all worked up about how crazy we are with them. Sorry, Hoss.

3 January 1991

Tired tonight. I don't feel like writing or drawing. I just feel like reading, which is easier and more relaxing. Still working on the bunker, odd tasks here and there, like finding out the number of certain items of equipment in each squadron, tasking them with projects, etc. It's been stormy lately. Yesterday it even rained a little bit.

I talked to Maryanne today; she sounded great and so happy to hear from me. I had strange dreams last night. I dreamed that she had changed, and I'm always thinking that I'm going to lose her somehow. I told her this on the phone, and she said not to worry, that I was just being silly. I guess being so far away is just making me scared and more concerned with things that I'm always taking for granted, like her being there for me and how much she loves me. It's too bad it takes something like this to make you think like that and not to take things so lightly.

I tried to build a table today that I could use to write on in the tent. There's a master sergeant and a lance corporal that are both good carpenters, and I was asking them how to go about it. Carpentry and construction are skills I have always wanted to be good at but have never had the time for. Lance Corporal Kutchner told me what I needed to lay down and plan out, and Top Riley, the senior enlisted Marine in the S-3, who is responsible for the daily operation of the office and is in charge of the work on our bunker, was also helping me out with pointers on how to get the table to sit even and solidly. Tomorrow I'll see where I can go with it.

I'm getting scared that this war is not going to go well for us and that they'll send Ryan over and straight to the front lines. I'm getting so morbid lately, thinking how fast life goes, how it seems just days ago that we were small kids safe in our parents' care and that now we are at an age where we can have kids of our own, where our parents are starting to look old, and where I'm thinking of my own mortality. I don't want to let life just fly on by, I almost want to grab it and slow it down. You keep wishing to get somewhere, and before you know it you're there, but your life is well spent. There is always so much to do and so much more to say to parents, siblings, spouse, and friends.

My grandmother died last year. She was so much to us, practically brought us up. A living, breathing, happy person, who had her own memories of a childhood with parents who protected her, of her girlhood, of romance, and of children. All that gone, completely buried. Her memories, hopes, pain, and aspirations, all gone. It's awful to be thinking like this. All you can do is not think of it, and just go on as if there will be no end. And even when you do that, it still sneaks up on you unawares. It's not the idea of death in combat or anything like that that has got me thinking this way, but probably just being so far away from home and having the time to stop and think about it all.

And the desert. The desert does funny things to you. It's no wonder three of the world's great religions were born in these deserts. Life is so elemental. Maybe that is where this is coming from. I'm starting to feel like Edgar Allen Poe or Baudelaire, morbidly possessed with the idea of death.

The only way to fight this is by laughing and forgetting all these morbid thoughts, so I'll wake Hoss up or start giving English a hard time. Crack a few jokes about the general's furniture or something, and then I'll be okay again. You got to be happy about stuff, make fun of things that bother you. That is the only way to enjoy this life that is flashing by so fast.

4 January 1991

Antsy tonight. Today I built my table and started on a chair. It was fun building it, and the table turned out quite well. It's really big, actually more of a drafting table than a writing table, but that is the way I like them. You can sit down and spread yourself out over it, feel the wood, and lose yourself in whatever you are doing. Now I just have to get it back to the tent.

Thinking about the work and building the table took me away from here for a while. The sun, the smell of sawed wood, the sawdust, and the iron nails. It's easy to forget things when you are working on something like that.

There is still a lot of talk about what is going to happen. About how effective or ineffective our air will be, about how long the war will last, or if we will be going to war at all. Saddam doesn't look as if he is going to back down, but who knows if we will really go through with it.

There was a lot of disagreement on the proper way to fortify the bunker today. Top Riley wants it one way, while English and I think it should be done another way. Who is right? None of us are engineers, so who is to say?

Top wants two layers of sandbags on top, and nothing else. I wanted to put one layer on, then put down another layer of wood on top of the sandbags. We would get the wood from the scrap lumber pile, where I got the wood to build my table, and there is more than enough long pieces there to do what I want with the bunker. I want the wood to be resting on the sandbag walls which are built up alongside the bunker, so that the weight from the wood, and the sandbags that would go on top of that, would be distributed not onto the top of the bunker, but onto the sandbags along the bunker walls. On top of the wood would be two more layers of sandbags, and then we would bury the whole thing under a pile of sand. I figure this would provide good cover and con-cealment, and I hope it would distribute the shock or force of any explosion in the general vicinity. Top thinks all this is unnecessary and would put too much weight on top of the bunker. He is afraid the roof will cave in and we will be trapped. In peacetime it would be a problem, but not a real big one. Now we really have to figure out the right way to do it because there is a great deal at stake.

I referred it to Captain O'Brien, who argued the same point with Top about the distribution of forces, but Top was adamant. I'm not sure if he doesn't under-stand, he's pretending not to understand, or if we are just wrong. Again this all boils down to a disagreement about what exactly the bunkers are supposed to do. Are they to protect us against a blast, which many people, Major Steven-son among them, say is a waste of time, or are they just for protection from shrapnel? Some people even think of them akin to a sort of fallout shelter where we can take cover and sit out a poison gas attack. We have stocked them with food and water for just this purpose, but I thought that with gas you wanted to get out of low lying areas, where it gathered. Another issue that we need guidance on.

In the end I let Top have his way. It's more important that he be allowed to make decisions and act accordingly than it is for me to implement a plan that I'm not even sure of. It's best not to take away his initiative.

Sometimes people perceive this as a leadership deficiency, almost passing off the control over a project, and they've probably perceived it in me. But in my situation, especially as a staff officer who doesn't really command troops, I think it is better to lead from a distance. Work alongside your people and watch how your SNCOs and NCOs lead them. Only step in if there is a major problem. This makes the Marines come to you. They have to find out what kind of officer you are, and they trust you more because you have been beside them before you have commanded them. Then when you do take charge and issue a command, you can do it easily and with the weight of authority.

Brand new second lieutenants dread the day they have to stand up in front of their men and take charge. They dread it because it puts them on the spot and makes them feel like they have to lay down the ground rules. But there is no rule that says you have to do it this way. I like to take command slowly. Watch how the staff sergeants and gunneys run the men, then as time goes by work myself into the organization. That way there is a mystery about me that wouldn't be there if I stood up front of them in the beginning and simply gave them the perfunctory motivational speech.

I should write Maryanne tonight, but I'm too tired. Probably wrote myself out with the journal. Eleven more days till the fifteenth, then I wonder what is going to happen.

8 January 1991

It's getting hard finding time to write, and this journal is becoming a stern taskmaster. I'll write down notes on small scraps of paper, and then save them until I get a chance to organize them all and put them all down. I'm getting obsessive about writing everything down, trying to capture what I'm seeing and feeling at every moment, and it's driving me crazy.

There is still not much to do at work, so we spend most of our time reading or writing letters. It's become a natural pattern. You work fast and well when something comes up but learn to relax and enjoy the time off when you have it. No need to think that there is a pattern to this, you just go with the flow.

Today was an easy day anyway. Just work on message traffic, more work on the bunkers, and a lot of reading. Right now we are waiting for Corporal Hall and Gunney Pescatore to finish with the engineer situation report, which of course they started working on at 1600, so Colonel Caldwell can sign it and get it off to Wing.

The S-3 shop is in charge of MWSG-37 operations. We all work for Colonel Caldwell, who reports directly to Colonel Coop, the CO. In the S-3, Major Stevenson is the S-3A, or assistant. Master Sergeant Riley is in charge of the day-to-day running of the shop and overseeing the enlisted personnel. Gunney Pescatore is the engineer coordinator, and Gunney Hendrix is the motor transport coordinator. Staff Sergeant James is the fuels coordinator. Sergeant Glenn is the NBC coordinator. On the admin side, are Sergeant McEntire and Sergeant Bose, who do most of the actual administrative work.

The S-3 also has a communications section. According to the T/O, all the Group rates is a comm coordinator, or liaison officer, but for whatever reason we have a full switchboard, run by a gunney and three troops. Finally there are the clerks and drivers, who double as both as needed. Lance Corporal Kutchner, Lance Corporal Scott, Corporal Hall, Hoss, and I round out this motley crew.

Yesterday John, Hall, and I went up to Manifah Bay. I'm taking every chance I get to get around this country, and so far I'm doing pretty well. Hall always seems sick of driving. He is the one who took us down to Bahrain the first time, but he is always ready to get the hell out of the office. He is also a chronic complainer, but that is just his way, and if you don't pay any attention to it he will do whatever you ask of him.

On the way to Manifah Bay, we saw a dead camel by the side of the road, which was sort of shocking in a strange way. Probably because of all the morbid thoughts I've been thinking about in the back of my mind and because of the value that the Arabs place on camels. To see it lying there, obviously hit by a car or truck, showed such tremendous disregard for the value of the camel's life.

There were a lot of troops on the move, and the bases up there that we visited seemed to be in the middle of nowhere. We went by the Direct Air Support Control (DASC) unit, which was way out in the middle of nothing on the Manifah Bay peninsula, and drove through a grunt camp to get there. I was psyched that I finally had a chance to see what the grunts were up to. It was their base camp, and they seemed to be doing almost the same thing as we were, getting ready for whatever was coming up. Lots of people, gear, and machinery all over the place. Huge lines at the phone centers and the Marines hanging out, "We're in the shit, man, just like they were in the 'Nam." The grunt camp seemed just as disorganized and crazy as it was at King Abdul Aziz, only more so, and the security at the gate was no better.

Anyway, I got to see the grunts, and, as always, I was wishing I was with them. I told John, and he told me what he always tells me: "Careful what you wish for, Hoss, you might get it. You're lucky your ass is right here and not with those poor bastards. All that glory bullshit, you want to just go get your ass shot off?"

Three days ago I took another trip, this time to Al Mishab. I went with Colonel Staunton, the Group XO, and Major Bacall, the adjutant. I asked if I could go after I heard they were going up there. Then I cleared it with Colonel Caldwell, and off I went. The more I see of everything the easier it will be to get around, and the more valuable I will be to the colonel.

Colonel Staunton was cool to travel with. He is a helo pilot, tall as hell, and an excellent officer. Everybody swears by him. He is very calm, very laid-back. I've never heard him get excited, but people jump when he tells them to do something. It showed in the way he traveled. Instead of just flying up there and back, we took our time, got our business done, then stopped by the ocean on the way back.

The beach seemed so beautiful, untouched, and forgotten. I found a few colored shells that I took to send home and what I thought was either some sort of fossil or the vertebrae off some fish. And the sea smell, just like home. It reminded me of Duxbury, of Plymouth and summers with my grandmother, and the Annapolis docks. It's so weird to keep thinking that we are preparing for war. That in a time when M.C. Hammer's dancing his ass off and Macintosh is bringing out a new line of computers, we have been sent off to the desert to fight hand to hand in trenches and mine fields, against a guy that just woke up one morning and decided to invade Kuwait.

Al Mishab is where MWSS-273 is going to set up shop. It's the closest that one of our units will be to the border, and they will move MAG-26 in there to provide helo support to the troops in the assault. Colonel Staunton went up to check out the place and check in with 273, which has already started moving up there. Al Mishab looks like what we expected to see coming over here. It's on the coast, and the water is just over a shallow rise, but there are dunes, sand, empty plains, the works.

Looking out over it all made me think of the deserts back home. Here everything is so bleak. Arabia is enchanting not because of the beauty of its deserts, but because of its history and spirit. The magnificent colors and vistas of the Southwest back home are much more beautiful, and so much more overwhelming. America is a land of immense space. What it must have felt like to be an early settler or an American Indian and to see all that spread out before you. A giant's country. And I think it's the sense of the mountains looming above it, and the canyons, that make it that way.

The Arabian deserts are just flat, lifeless, and plain, with here and there blown sand piled up in dunes that look like the deserts did in *Lawrence of Arabia*. This is really the only thing there is to break up the emptiness of the desert around you. It just stretches out to a dirty, dingy horizon, and the dry, hard taste of it lingers in your mouth.

I moved my table and chair to the tent today. The table takes up enough space, and I'm not sure how happy everyone was to have it in there, but I love it. I just moved my cot to fit underneath the table top, and that really takes up no more room than I had before.

"Man, Sean, think the thing's big enough?"

I also finally got mail today. Just took a while I guess. I got three letters from Maryanne, one with pictures. Damn, it made me feel good to see her, she looked great.

Other projects today: building fighting tops on top of the bunkers. What the hell those are for I have no idea. A last stand? Putting cammie netting all over the HQ, which is good for cover and really cools the place down but a real pain in the ass for the troops who have to readjust it every morning after the wind blows the stuff all over the place during the night.

And notes: remember when you lead men, it's not enough to keep them busy. You have to keep them challenged, so that they grow as well.

Grunts get two meals of hot chow a day at the base camp, or logistics support camp as it's called, where they rest between trips out to the desert.

Right now they are in a maintenance stand-down period, getting ready for whatever is coming up.

Just like us. Waiting, restless, moving around, thinking about home. I always tend to think that things are so much more exciting in the other units or branches of the Marine Corps, when most of the time all anybody is doing around here is waiting. You have to get the most out of where you are. There are advantages and disadvantages to being anywhere, just quit thinking that every place else is so much better or more involved.

The guard at the 273 entry post, a female lance corporal, talking to Lieutenant Colonel Staunton:

"Which way to 273?"

"That's my unit! Hah!"

"Yea, well we're looking for it."

"Just go through there."

Great first line of defense for MWSS-273, especially so close to the border.

MWR was giving out Walkmen and TVs the other day. Stringing cammie net over the tops of the bunkers instead of just dumping sand over them. Any difference? Maybe the cammie should go over the pile of sand?

Complaints about the inability of the CSSD's (Combat Service Support Detachment) to support the MWSSs. CSSD is the lowest level of support on the FSSG side. It is where the rubber meets the road and where units go to get everything they need to function, like parts. Word is that they are having trouble supporting us because of a lack of essential parts.

In short supply: bunker material, sandbags, tactical wire (concertina, etc.), engineer stakes, repair parts (for forklifts, generators, etc.), tents (everybody is short tents — Colonel Coop has an armed guard on the ones we haven't distributed yet so we can keep other Wing units, the FSSG, and even the Division from stealing them), ROWPU (Reverse Osmosis Water Purification Unit) chemicals (which were supposed to be stored with the ROWPU units on the

MPS ships, but weren't. The ROWPUs came off without any chemicals at all. So how are we supposed to purify the damn water?).

Enough notes for tonight. I'll try and finish updating tomorrow. Also have to try and catch up with my letter writing.

11 January 1991

Today has been a pretty good day so far. Major Stevenson gave us a brief this morning, for the whole S-3, about what is going on in the big picture. I think he did this because everybody in the S-3 was complaining about not knowing what was going on. The major explained the concept of operations as of this moment and made us all feel a little more a part of what is happening. Needless to say it was a tremendous morale booster. He even gave us a hint of what it was we were supposed to be doing for the S-3 on a day-to-day basis.

Psyched up, we all went back to work with a new sense of purpose.

Yesterday I rode up to 1/12, an artillery unit, with Corporal Hall and Sergeant Glenn to trade gas masks for MOPP boots. We needed MOPP boots and had extra gas masks, so Sergeant Glenn had arranged a trade with one of his buddies in 1/12's NBC section, who needed the gas masks. We went back up to the Manifah Bay logistics camp, where Sergeant Glenn was supposed to meet this guy, and found out they were all in the field. Then out into the desert to find the battalion itself, and we hoped, Sergeant Glenn's buddy.

The main highway runs right up along the coast. To get out on the Manifah Bay peninsula you go right. Then to get out to where 1/12 was we had to go further north and then turn left onto a barely discernable dirt road and head out into the desert. We found 1/12 just as we were told we would. They were in the middle of nowhere, and it was kind of weird being out there. Just the unit, some Marines digging in, the cold winds blowing off the desert, and the horizon stretching off to nothing in every direction. Just an empty expanse of shallow hills and sand.

The guards were living in holes dug into the sand with ponchos or shelter halves stretched out above them to keep the wind out. If they were lucky, they had a cot to put their sleeping bags on. Man, did they look miserable. Playing cards, just sitting around staring blankly. All of them were cold, much colder than we ever were at King Abdul Aziz.

The rest of the battalion was dug in behind some shallow hills. Their artillery pieces were all pointed north, and you could tell that everybody was pretty excited with the deadline approaching and all. The batteries were split up, but we found Sergeant Glenn's buddy easily enough at their headquarters battery.

We got the boots and headed off home. I kept looking behind us as we went. The sun was setting, and the Marines just waited there, dug in, for whatever was coming.

Gunney Harlan, the S-2, or intelligence officer for MWSG-37, is a hard man to figure out. Antisocial, angry, and unevenly tempered, if not openly disrespectful, he doesn't seem to get along with anybody. Why the command puts up with him I can't even begin to guess. He never returns anybody's greeting, never says hello to anybody, and always seems in a bad mood. This is not the way a leader of Marines should act in a high stress environment. He needs to be somebody you can look up to and depend on, not an asshole who has a problem with the world.

He got in a fistfight with another gunney, whom he almost killed, a little while back, and he has almost pushed Tony over the edge a few times. Tony is an ex-drill instructor and a long-time infantryman. If there is anywhere you better know what respect and leadership mean, it's in the grunts, and I know this gunney is really pissing him off.

Every night we have guards posted around the headquarters area who are responsible for safeguarding equipment and for security around the area. They are mostly young troops, tired, bored, maybe scared, but alert and trustworthy. They are supposed to challenge anybody they don't know or recognize; that is part of the general orders of a sentry. One night about dusk one of the S-3 clerks on duty, Lance Corporal Scott, challenged Gunney Harlan, whom he couldn't make out in the shadows. Gunney Harlan not only refused the challenge, but promptly chewed Scott out, explaining to him that this was not proper security procedure.

Gunney Harlan used the weight of his authority and position to undermine this kid carrying out his duties properly and aggressively. Not only was Scott right in challenging him, but even if he was wrong, the gunney should have done as he was told by the sentry. A sentry's authority is unquestionable. And why temper that diligence? Why put the idea into that young Marine's head that he is being too aggressive? You want young firebreathers taking charge and being hard, that is the way they should be. Fucking gunney. I told Scott the next time somebody refused his challenge he should just shoot him.

I also took Lance Corporal Kutchner to the hospital today to get her tested for pregnancy. She'd gone to the clinic here at the stadium twice, and each time they told her she wasn't pregnant. But she's getting heavier, more run down, and a little sick in the mornings. She also said that she feels as she did when she had her last baby. Kutchner is an excellent Marine, and I had a feeling she was pregnant, but that for some reason the clinic tests weren't showing it. So I decided to take her to the hospital to find out for sure, especially since the deadline is just days off now, and if she is pregnant, she has got to get the hell out of here.

I told Colonel Caldwell we were going, and he said no problem. The hospital is at the port, so I drove Kutchner up there, asked that they do a pregnancy test and waited outside while they did it. It was kind of funny, I almost felt like a father or something waiting for the word. I wondered if they thought the kid was mine. Naah.

The facilities themselves were great. Giant tents with fancy ventilation systems to keep out germs and dust, plenty of room, and good people. Kutch came out in about ten minutes, and we went to lunch at the hospital chow hall while waiting for the results. The food was great, and plenty of it, and when we got back they had the news. Kutchner was pregnant.

I was happy for her, but sorry to be seeing her go. We would definitely miss her. She had just taken over the motor transport dispatching job from Gunney Hendrix and had done outstanding work getting it organized, and here she would be leaving in no time at all. Poor Hendrix, he was a disaster with paperwork and organizing things. And poor us, now he could go back to his old ways of trading our vehicles to people for things he needed or wanted.

This episode also made me think about women in the Marine Corps. My mother is a strong woman, and maybe because of her I've always thought women should have the right to do anything that anybody else could. But what do you do if you have these women in the military, whom you depend on, and then they get sent home because they are pregnant? Is that fair? But then again, can you deprive women of the right to be pregnant in the military?

Lieutenant Colonel Staunton was selected today for colonel, which psyched me up because he deserved it. I got psyched too about Captain Howard, he got promoted to major. Actually he's been frocked, which means that even though you are not getting paid at a certain rank, you can wear it because you have been selected for it and you will get the promotion in the future. This is at the CO's imperative and gives Captain, now Major, Howard, more power to get things done as the Group S-4. Lieutenant Colonel Staunton, on the other hand, still has to wait to get promoted, but now it's just a matter of time, since he has already been selected.

When I congratulated Colonel Staunton on his promotion he looked kind of dazed and told me that he had never imagined he would be making the Marine Corps a career, that he would be a colonel and in for the long haul. I said that he must have done a good job as a squadron CO, and he said no, that it was actually the staff jobs that got you promoted. You got a reputation from the people you worked for, and how well you did for them would determine the extent and success of your career. I never thought about that. I guess this job ain't so bad after all. I guess you can make things happen for the big guys that are really accomplishing something.

Yesterday I got two letters from my mother. Made me happy as hell, and I loved the stamps she sent them with. They were movie stamps, one of *Beau Geste*, the other of *Stagecoach*. They really made me homesick, more than even the letters themselves. After reading my mother's letter I didn't feel so bad about the one I sent my parents a few days ago. Boy was it corny. I guess you can't help but feel and write that way in this sort of situation. It really makes you think back on a lot of stuff. Makes everything take on a whole different light.

The kid who took Sergeant Glenn and me up to 1/12, a lance corporal, told me he had never put on a MOPP suit before. I asked him if he knew how to do it in case he had to, and he told me that he thought so because they had "shown us how." This struck me as kind of funny. I wonder who the NBC officer was in his unit. The time to learn how to put on a MOPP suit is not when it's a matter of life and death. And how is he supposed to do it with any degree of confidence and control in the midst of a chemical attack if he is not even sure how to do it? I hope this kid is an exception to what I've thought was a first class NBC training program throughout the Marine Corps.

The artillery battalion we visited, 1/12, was having comm troubles when we pulled up there. I guess this is typical. We definitely have comm troubles at 37 and throughout the Wing. We can talk to anyone in the United States whenever we feel like it, but we can't call MWSS-174 a hundred yards down the road.

We also got our anthrax shots a few days back. This is for any biological weapons, specifically anthrax, that Saddam might use against us. I don't know how much good it will do. I've heard that doctors are saying the shots need to be administered about six months in advance and that once administered they only work against one strain of the virus, when there are millions out there that will kill you. Oh, well. Maybe it's just to make us feel better anyway. Sometimes I think almost everything they do is just to make us feel better.

The shots were actually pretty painful as far as shots go. They poked a big long needle into your hip just above the ass and injected the fluid in. You could feel it going in, thick and hot, and the area stayed tender for a day or two. They say we have to get a new anthrax shot every two months, which is not something I'll be looking forward to.

I talked to Top Riley about the shots. He is still very bitter about Agent Orange in Vietnam and doesn't see any good in these shots or the pills we will be taking to counteract the effects of any nerve agent we might be exposed to. Sometimes I'm even less convinced than he is about how safe all this crap is, or if it's even worth the effort.

13 January 1991

Two days to go until the deadline runs out. Today was quiet. Really the only thing I had to do was find out about some NBC canisters which were missing from a few ROWPU units that the squadrons have. The canisters are SL-3 components of the ROWPU, so they should have been with them, but they weren't. Now we have to find out what they are exactly so we can replace them. They enable you to keep making water in a contaminated environment, and about half the ROWPUs we have are missing them, so everybody is pretty gung ho about getting them replaced.

Yesterday morning I went to the port with Jerry and Tony looking for trucks and transportation. They do this all the time, and man, what a pain in the ass it is. Of course there are none to be had, and you end up just wasting your time and getting nothing for it. The morning was a bust, and we left empty-handed.

Getting trucks is a big deal. Everybody has things they need to get moved before Tuesday, and nobody has enough assets to do it themselves. That is what the motor transport companies are for. The army has entire divisions that do nothing but motor transport, where the Marine Corps has battalions and companies to do the job. When a unit needs something moved, they first see if they can do it using internal assets. Front line units, like the flying squadrons or the grunts, go to their commands to request transportation. The commands provide it, or if they can't, go to the next higher level to get what's needed. You always want to preserve your own assets for emergencies and to keep the wear and tear down on them, so a good unit will use external transportation as much as possible.

External transportation usually comes out of the FSSG. That is where all the big vehicles are and where they run the motor pools from. Our FSSG works out of the port, and if you need vehicles, that is where you have to go. You submit a request to the FSSG motor transport people, wait for them to prioritize your mission, then if you're lucky, you pick up the trucks the next day at the port and use them to haul whatever it is you are hauling. You only have to provide the driver and get the vehicle back on time when you are done with it.

The trouble is, there are just not enough trucks to go around. We have contracted out with the Saudi government to get a whole bunch of tractor trailers with Saudi-supplied drivers, but there still aren't nearly enough trucks to move everything that needs to be moved. The Division gets first priority, and everybody else comes after. So day after day the Wing and FSSG get low priorities and either get the trucks late, or not at all. It's all very frustrating to say the least.

We just don't have the assets we need to move everything. It's bad enough we are depending on the civilian trucks so much. Who is to say if they will even stick around when things get rough? But you do what you have to do, and you learn quickly to look out for yourself because if you don't no one else will. Everybody's mission is important; it's the guy who hustles the most that will get what he needs.

Later Jerry and Tony went back up to the port, found out the name of the army unit that did have a high priority but hadn't showed up yet, and then made off with their trucks, claiming to be the army reps. That is just the sort of thing you have to do. Part of it is the system they have to give the trucks out. Once you get your priority the FSSG people give you a time for the next morning. If you don't show up, they give you two hours, then they call to remind you that you have trucks waiting. Then, after waiting another two hours for the people to show up, they might think about reassigning the vehicles, which have just sat there the whole morning. If the trucks are that damned important to get such a high priority why aren't the people there to pick them up at first light? It happens all the time, and many times the units with the high priorities just don't even show. So to hell with them, we'll just swipe the trucks.

Then to keep the trucks, you just don't turn them back in after you are done with them for the night. You will need them again, so why not just hang on to them? We did this, so the FSSG people at the port started sending their own A-drivers out with each truck. These guys were supposed to make sure that the trucks got back to the port. Motor transport battalion must have lost at least half of their tractor trailers before they started doing this. So it ended up being a constant battle between the motor transport people at the port and other units over the control of the tractor trailers. Then there is the problem of the Saudi drivers that you have to deal with once you get your hands on the trucks.

This is a dangerous development. We depend so much on this civilian transportation to move our equipment, supplies, ammunition, tanks, and everything else we need to keep the forward units moving, and the trucks are starting to disappear with their civilian drivers as the threat of war approaches. I wonder if we will be able to keep things moving if it does start up.

And finally tonight, when I told Captain O'Brien about the possibility of germ warfare, he replied: "You've got to be kidding me. When is it enough already?"

15 January 1991

Today is the day. Everybody is curious if and when we will attack. I'm betting on the eighteenth, but I hope it's tonight. Yesterday and the day before, it rained constantly, and all of our computers and comm gear started going bust with the rain leaking through the walls and down through the ceilings. It was strange it raining so much in the desert. Everything is so damp. I also had a migraine come on the night before last. God, I hate them. You can feel them coming, and they hit usually in the middle of the night, after only a few hours of troubled sleep.

I woke up in pain, alone in my misery, and lay there for about a half an hour, trying to relax and get control of it. The tent was quiet. Everybody else was still asleep. At about midnight I got up and went to the showers. They were completely deserted, a far cry from the way they are all day and through the evening, packed with people waiting in line for a turn in the bathroom and under the shower. I took a long, hot shower, then cleaned out my soap dish and used it to take the Alka Seltzer I kept in my toilet bag for just this reason. Alka Seltzer is the only thing I know of that gets rid of the migraine for me. I drank a lot of water and was feeling better immediately.

Maybe I was dehydrated. Maybe I was worrying too much about things.

I went back to the tent, laid down, and tried to relax. After about twenty minutes of quiet reflection, I finally fell asleep again, and this time I slept the deep, long, and restful sleep that comes after the migraines go away. The next morning I was just so happy to be feeling good again that I reminded myself to quit getting worked up about things.

Yesterday spent the day writing a rapid runway repair LOI.

Jerry and Tony also told me it's getting harder for them to get trucks. There are just no more to be had. All the civilian truck drivers are taking off with their trucks with the coming of the deadline. There are no ships coming into the port anymore; the weather has been too bad the last few days for them to dock. The staging of the EAF equipment is delayed for the same reason, the bad weather.

There have been reports of terrorist activity. They found direction markers near the steel fence at the ASP in Bahrain, and everybody has been told to stay on the lookout for anything unusual. Uniforms have been missing from the civilian laundry, and the laundry itself closed down shop today to clear out of town before the war kicks off, if it kicks off.

Lance Corporal Kutchner finally got out of here. She left yesterday. Bet her husband can't wait to see her.

I went with Major Howard up to 3D MAW today. They are now at Jubail Airport, having moved up from Bahrain for whatever is coming. He was trying to get BPA authority granted to the Group from a Wing supply officer, a real butt-head. I don't know why, but many times people in admin and supply act like the frigging Marine Corps money is their own and shortchange the people who need it all the time. There is nothing wrong with being responsible about the Marine Corps's money, but there is when you start making it hard for other Marines to get their jobs done.

The colonel up at Wing didn't want the Group to have BPA authority because he didn't trust us. "BPA authority is intended for administrative and personnel supplies, not parts, which is what everybody is using it for. Everybody has to start using the FSSG and the CSSDs for parts. We need to get usage data on all this stuff, and too many people use the BPA anyways. There is too much paperwork on everything, we're way behind. There are payments behind, claims not filled, and the Saudi economy in this area has been cleaned out. We keep having to move further out to get the stuff we need."

This all sounds good, but he is talking out his ass. The FSSG and CSSD aren't coming through with the supplies, so all the units are getting them out in town the only way they know how, with the BPA, but at least they are getting them. There is a good argument for forcing the system to work and making the units use the CSSDs, even if they go short on parts for a while, to get it running. But this is asking a bit much. Support is supposed to be easy and dependable. You are not supposed to have to "make it work."

He is also off when he says they don't get usage data when they open purchase things on the BPA. They record it and it hits the prints just as anything does they would get through the system. Again, it's all a question of control and trusting the lowest unit possible to get the job done right. They have decentralized command and control in the combat arms, it's one of the basic tenents our whole philosophy of war fighting is built on. When are they going to do this in the support sections?

Our next stop was the G-4, to see about a problem one of our squadrons was having with an ammunition request. MWSS-273 is low on ammunition. As units come in country, they receive an initial issue that is expected to last until they get resupplied. MWSS-273 never received their initial issue, and Major Howard is trying to make sure they get the ammo they need.

This is how the system works, as well as I can make out: The unit needing the initial supply of ammunition turns in a weapons density list to its parent command, which then decides how much ammunition the unit will get. When MWSS-273 first deployed to Saudi Arabia, its parent command was 3D MAW. Like every other support squadron in country, MWSS-273 initially fell directly beneath the Wing and provided support directly to its respective MAG.

After the parent command decides how much ammunition the requesting unit needs, which in this case is the 3D MAW deciding what MWSS-273 needed, the command would draft up a message requesting that ammo allowance be issued directly to the unit. This message would go to I MEF for endorsement, and I MEF would direct the FSSG to dole it out at the respective ammunition supply point, or ASP. I guess this works well enough with the ground units, but in the Wing all the ASPs are run by Marine aviation logistics squadrons, which don't fall under the direct control of the FSSG.

So what was MWSS-273 supposed to do? MALS wouldn't give them a resupply of ammo because they hadn't expended any, and there was no reason for the FSSG to give it to them because the MALS was responsible for supplying all Wing units. So MWSS-273 was hanging out at Al Mishab with less than a round per man, waiting for the Iraqis to come rolling down the road, all because they had failed to get their initial supply of ammunition and couldn't get any now to make up for it.

To correct the problem, MWSG-37 needed to fire off a message to the 3D MAW explaining the problem and requesting the release of an amount of small arms ammo which would equal the initial allowance. This is what was taking forever to get done. The major just didn't seem in any kind of a hurry to get it through. As he said, "If ammo requests are different from requests on file at the main ASP, you need to send a letter back to CMC requesting action." (And this on the 13th of January.) "Then there'll be a forty-eight-hour wait for the request to clear."

I was shocked at all this, thinking once again that everything was all screwed up, but maybe that is just the way all junior officers feel when they see the system in action. Maybe everything seems screwed up because it seems to move so slowly, and junior officers and troops just expect things to move fast. Perhaps it is impatience and misguided expectations on our part. I'm just not sure. Major Howard never gets that worked up about it. As he said: "Things are working okay. If they weren't, there would be no ammo to be had."

It is amazing that how anything gets done around here. Nothing seems to progress in any kind of natural or planned order. It just seems to happen. Things move along at their own slow pace until you finally have what you need. But there is no rushing it. Making things happen is like trying to move an elephant; the best you can do is to set it in motion and hope it keeps moving, maybe pressing it here and there to go one way or the other, but never really controlling it.

Who is actually in charge of the air station? And who is responsible for its defense? Is it the MAG commander? The MALS commander? The MWSS commander?

Seems to me that having the MAG commander in charge of the air station defense is rather like having an aircraft carrier captain in charge of the defense of the aircraft carrier. He is in charge of launching the planes on missions and controlling the carrier battle group that serves to support him. He doesn't concern himself with shooting off the vulcan-phalanx gatling guns or the ship's anti-aircraft batteries. These missions would distract him from his real job: engaging the enemy with the carrier battle group and his aircraft.

So why should an air station commander be in charge of air station defense and security measures? Give those tasks to the support squadron. It should be a ground support requirement. Let the MWSS work out a security system and tie all the units on the airfield into it. Establish an HQ, a reaction force, and a real plan to fight ground, terrorist, or saboteur assault. I don't see this at any of the air stations now.

16 January 1991

The day after the deadline, which actually expired at 0800 this morning, and nothing has happened. Just waiting as usual.

The LOI on rapid runway repair is signed and ready to go. The colonel made only a few corrections to it, so I guess it turned out pretty well. Let's hope the people who read it think so. Now just making copies of it to get out to the other commands.

17 January 1991

A lot of stuff to get down. Yesterday Colonel Coop came in happy, then at 0800 suddenly demanded that the sergeant major complete the sandbag wall around the tents that he had told him to get up a week earlier. "I want it done, now!"

So we all fell to on the sandbags, everybody. All day shoveling, filling, tying, transporting, and stacking. An hour break for dinner and then back on with engineer lights until 2200.

We saw aircraft ammunition being brought out, and it looked as if they were finally going to do it. I hopped in Colonel Staunton's Jeep Cherokee on the way back up the road to the HQ, just about a hundred yards, and he confirmed it. "Tonight's the night."

Yea, buddy!

At 2200 we had a formation. It was dark and quiet. The CO was very calm, very much like a father. No big deal, nothing to get worried about, just what was coming up. He told us that the thing he feared most wasn't scud missiles, or terrorists, or saboteurs, but other Marines and the hell that would break loose in a panic at night. That is what the sandbags around the tents were for. If something happened, we were to roll off our cots and lie on the floor with our gas masks near by. We were to stay relaxed, under the level of the sandbag wall, not nervous or itchy to do anything. Then we were to go back to sleep, on the floor, and let the rest of the camp get control of itself.

What would happen if anybody heard a shot fired at night? Or if terrorists or commandos did infiltrate the camp? All they would have to do was make a disturbance, and the Marines would take care of the rest. There would be rifles going off, pistols, Marines shooting at each other, in a word, chaos. But we would just sit it out, under the sandbags, safe and ready for the next day. Colonel Coop was right, of course. Every Vietnam vet I've ever spoken to says that it isn't really the bad guys you need to worry about, it is everyone and everything else that will get you before the enemy does.

So we went back to our tents. Expectant, excited, nervous, and feeling kind of strange. I laid my stuff out as I got ready for bed so I could follow instructions: "Just roll out of your cots onto the ground and have a drink of water. Then put on your gas mask and wait." I laid out my flak jacket to roll into, my NBC gear, my mask, and my pistol. Then I went and took a shower, carrying my pistol and gas mask with me, as always. The shower was quiet, not that many people were in there so late. "What would I do if we had a scud attack now?" I was thinking to myself as the warm water washed over my body. Fuck it, who cares.

It was hard trying to get to sleep, but I was tired from the day's work and eventually drifted off.

The radio was in my dreams. Something was happening. I woke up. It was dark, and I didn't know who else was awake, but it was clear from the news that the war had started. The first group of planes had taken off and were dropping their bombs on Baghdad. A thrill ran through me, and I felt like yelling out to see who else was awake, but I didn't. It was exciting, and very, very weird just to be lying there and following the air assault on the radio while everything else around me seemed so calm and uneventful. We were at war. For real, a goddamned war, and I was fighting in it.

Suddenly, maybe after about fifteen minutes or so, I think, Captain O'Brien yelled out, "They've attacked!" and Jerry and Tony jumped up to get dressed. It was still early, about 0300 or 0400, but we were all too excited to go on sleeping. They ran out and went to watch the TV in the stadium basement, while John got up to take a whiz. "You're a veteran now, Caleb." Damn, I couldn't believe it.

A goddamned war! Then slowly I fell asleep again.

When I awoke again, the radio was really loud, and we listened to it intently as we got up as usual and went to breakfast.

On my way out of the showers last night, I saw Captain Tom Kennedy from 31st Company at USNA. He flies Harriers now, and he is in one of the squadrons that is based at King Abdul Aziz. I said hi, asked him what was up and if he was involved in whatever was going on the next day.

He told me that the AV-8B Harrier strikes planned for early that morning had been scrapped because they didn't have the EA-6B assets to support the mission. They were on for the day after, but the higher-ups also wanted to preserve them for close air support when they'd really need them, which is their primary mission, so those missions might get scrapped as well. The Air Force wanted them used because they were so close to the border and easy to bring on target, but since they didn't have the EA-6B assets to support them, the Air Force would just have to wait.

Tom sounded pretty disappointed, to say the least. But he was pretty sure they would get their chance, sooner or later.

Today we continued with the sandbags and listened to a blow-by-blow account of the battle, cheering and rooting for the pilots after each reported attack. I waved at a few of the Harriers as they flew back in, coming in right over us where we were filling our sandbags at the end of the runway.

It's weird being able to follow the whole thing as it happens, and a little scary. It doesn't even seem as if we are actually at war right now. It all seems so unreal.

With all our seemingly phenomenal success, I can't figure out what the hell Saddam Hussein is trying to do. He keeps talking big, even now, but he is getting his ass kicked. He hasn't attacked Israel, has only put up a haphazard resistance to the air attacks, and Baghdad wasn't even blacked out until half an hour into the air assault. I thought for sure once he knew we were going in he would launch everything he had at all our defensive and supporting positions and at Israel, to drag them into this, if it took everything he had to do it. But he hasn't done anything. I kept picturing a scenario where he would saturate preplanned targets with a Soviet-style barrage of weapons and missiles, setting us back for a bit and killing as many of us as possible, to set America and Americans back a step wondering if all this was worth it. But it just hasn't happened. What the hell is he waiting for?

Maybe he is just banking on a decisive ground war. Last night Tom said that this might be a battle that could be won entirely from the air — for the first time in history. Then tonight I talked to a forward observer, an 03, whose job it is to fly as an FO for a pilot in an OV-10 Bronco and report everything he sees about enemy positions, capabilities, and basically all other intelligence information that might be of use to the other pilots or to ground troops. It's an 03 billet because the FO uses his infantry expertise to analyze what he sees on the ground. He said it was pretty wild up there, silent, with just the black bursts of flack whipping by outside. I asked him how effective our bombing would be on the enemy ground positions, which are supposed to be dug in so well, and he said to knock out the various positions of either tanks, or infantry, or artillery, it takes a direct hit on top of the position by at least a 10,000 pound bomb. He added: "A bomber has to fly down the line of entrenchments and make a direct hit on the position to knock any of those Iraqi ground units out. If air can knock out the Iraqi artillery positions, the grunts'll be okay. If not, they're going to get creamed."

Doesn't sound too good. If Saddam can keep his forces buried and withstand the air assaults, maybe he will have enough left to knock the momentum off of any ground offensive we might have planned. If he can kill enough soldiers in the offensive, maybe that will give him a reprieve while the U.S. begins to debate the wisdom of its policies over here. I know for sure that if the American people start seeing on the news casualty figures of tens of thousands lost in a single day, there are gonna be some questions asked and maybe a loss of will. Maybe that is what Saddam is banking on.

The pilots are definitely pumped. They are coming back from their missions different men. At dinner they are still all juiced up, and they are talking all the time about what it's like up there. They will tell you if you ask them; it's almost like they are on speed or something. Their adrenalin must be going crazy. Tom said it's unbelievable. He can't believe that he is flying actual combat missions. He said he was nervous as hell at first flying in, but once they start doing what they have been trained to do, instinct takes over. They quit thinking about everything, and before they know it they are on their way back. Man, now I wish I had been a pilot.

I also found out one of our arty battalions suppressed one of their positions already. Way to go — rockin' and rollin' all over those dudes.

It's late now, and time to get some rest. I'm tired, but feeling good. I'm sunburnt and clean after my shower and just listening to the radio to unwind. What other war has been so fully and immediately presented? Talk about keeping the troops informed. It doesn't matter if the higher ranks do that or not now, we probably know just as much as they do about what is going on because of all these intrepid CNN reporters. Man, what a wacko war.

18 January 1991

Another strange night last night. Yesterday everybody was talking on the news as if we had won the war already, and last night we woke up to the sound of air raid sirens coming over the radio and the news that Iraq had hit Israel with a number of scud missiles, reminding us that this is long from over. Then we heard shots, and instantly the whole tent was up and ready, for what we had no idea.

Somebody on the flight line had had an accidental discharge, which set off a whole bunch of shots in reply. I chambered a round, much to everyone else's annoyance, then sat back and waited. A bit later we heard another air raid siren, far off, which we could barely make out. It was the Jubail civil defense siren, and we scrambled to get our NBC gear ready once we realized what it was. Luckily it was a false alarm.

Only later did I find out what had really happened. A car had driven by an MP HUMMV on patrol and had supposedly backfired as it went past. The MPs roared off in pursuit of the vehicle, thinking that it was a bunch of terrorists or something. The HUMMV was cruising down the road after the car when it hit a pretty big bump, causing the 50 cal gunner in the back to jerk forward and squeeze off a string of rounds. These impacted harmlessly on the ground in front of the HUMMV, but they ended up losing the car anyway. I guess the air raid siren was a civilian alarm warning of another of Saddam's inbound scud missiles. Whenever they are launched now, the sirens go off. They probably figure it is safer that way. Too bad they have usually impacted before we can even hear the sirens.

The radio is always there, drifting in and out of our consciousness. The very idea of it being so live is changing the whole nature of the conflict. It gives us immediate, excellent intelligence. It is hypnotic, and yet at the same time, you get a sense that it is really missing out on some things. It adds this strange, surreal dimension to everything. Last night I was thinking how ironic it is that Saddam Hussein, a man with intimate connections in the shadow world of international terrorism, who of all people should know and understand the nature of the media, should be so badly used by it.

Terrorists have supposedly written the doctrine on media manipulation and are said to be experts in the abilities to hold the Western world hostage by its own free press. But like everything else in our world, I guess the experts have taken note of this, and many of their strategies have become entrenched at the highest levels of our own government and national institutions. It is so funny now to see the tables turned and our boys making use of the media like there is no tomorrow. Saddam is being humiliated again and again at the hands of our news services. They are reporting things that they are almost making come about.

The news stations are starved for news and grab at anything they can report. So they spit out whatever they can glean on the progress of the war.

Faint rumblings they have heard in Pentagon hallways, rumors, speculation. It becomes the material for the newscast, is reported, then in the dearth of any new information it gets reported again and again. Updated, maybe confirmed, maybe not. But with gaining momentum and the force of repetition, the news takes on a life of its own and actually becomes the truth. Arabs always fight on the side which looks as if it is going to win; they blow with the wind until they can sense the prevailing direction. So this type of news builds right into our hands. The Iraqis might already think the war is over because CNN is reporting it that way. Eat your heart out Walter Cronkite — we are doing it the way it should be done. Don't let the bastards know anything. I just hope we aren't fooling ourselves.

Everybody thinks it is going well. Wall Street had a big surge yesterday, and by all accounts we have been doing great so far, with unbelievably light losses. I think Saddam is just waiting for his chance. He will gamble it all on a wild throw of the dice, trying to smash our ground assault and throw the media right back in our face. He will bring all the news reportage over to his side and bring our efforts to a standstill.

I think we did catch him by surprise, for whatever reason, but he will be ready when we throw our ground forces into the fray. (Would it have been even better to attack that night with our ground trops as well, in one all-out ferocious attack?) I still don't understand why he waited to attack Israel. But he is finally doing it, as I would have done if I were him. He has got to hit Israel hard, drag them into this, dig in, and wait.

Got three letters this morning. Two from Maryanne and one from her parents. Now I'm just bored. Life seems as if it is back to normal if you just switch off the damned news.

We are taking the NBC pills now to prepare our nervous systems for the atropine injections if we get attacked with nerve gas. They must be affecting me because I'm drowsy, nauseous, feeling sick, and getting very, very depressed.

I hate thinking that I am ever missing out on anything, that I can't experience something, or that I am not making the most of my life. I hate that feeling more than anything. And here I sit now, in impotent anger, while the war rages around me. I guess I am lucky enough to have made it over here ... ahh, frustration!

Whoosh! Another plane roars down the runway right outside the window and takes off for Iraq. And another, and still another.

We are watching General Schwarzkopf's briefing, with Air Force Lieutenant General Horner and a bunch of photos and videos of the operation so far. Another plane is warming up on the flight line as we are drifting off to sleep.

19 January 1991

Last night was a real wild one. I had bad vibes all day that we would be hit that night, and that is almost what happened. It started with my going up to

Jubail Airport with Jerry Healey and Tony Rominger. They were trying to grab the three pallets that were due in as they came off the planes, but they ended up only getting one. The planes that were supposed to be delivering the pallets had been warned off. You landed at your own risk at night because of the scud threat, and most of the pilots didn't want to chance it.

Once they found the one pallet, they radioed back for a truck to get it home, and we piled in the Blazer to talk, joke, and pass the time while we waited.

We were just taking it easy, joking about everyone else being back in their racks asleep while we were up doing this shit, when I noticed a bunch of guys running out of the rec tent, where the TV was, and heading for the bunkers. Scuds! We jumped out of the Blazer, grabbed our gear out of the back of it, and ran to try to find the nearest bunker. We followed everybody else and found ourselves in a small bunker, crowded in with about six other people. The bunker was divided in two by the wooden beams which held up the roof, and it had benches running around the sides of it. It looked like a pretty solid, safe bunker.

First off we began to don and clear. No problem, just do it as you have been trained to do. Good enough for the Marines.

The poor Air Force guys were going crazy. I don't know if it was lack of training or just panic, but they were scrambling around out of breath, doing nothing as they were supposed to. They were each in various stages of putting their MOPP suits on, yet none of them had their gas mask on. Tony was busy putting his own mask on when he stopped to watch them, incredulous. "What the hell are you guys doing?" he asked.

Another guy appeared from up top, breathing hard. He had all his MOPP gear, but he'd forgotten his mask.

After the all clear sounded, we went back out to the Blazer to wait again, now with something new to joke about. Over Tony's hand held radio, we asked about the truck. It was on its way. It has been on its way for two hours now. Oh well, nothing to do but wait.

Finally at about 0030 the truck showed up. We had the driver take the canvas off and put one side down, then had a forklift load the one pallet on board. The driver and his A-driver put the side back up and took off for King Abdul Aziz.

I drove the Blazer back, while Jerry and Tony fell asleep, exhausted.

When we got home and arrived at the tent, we made a racket going in to wake everybody up. Jerry and Tony had already agreed to drop their helmets on the floor in tandem as they went by English's bed, which proved loud enough to jar the whole tent awake. Everybody pretended to ignore it, and we just kept on making noise. This had a variety of effects over the next few hours, as Richard rose to the assault. He got up after we had settled in and made his own noise, then went out to the head. I was pissed at that and threw his prized chair across the room while he was gone.

When Richard came back, he blamed Tony for the chair, of course, since everybody always blames Tony for everything. He just has that look. Things did settle down a bit until morning, but then Tony and Richard almost got into it. I tend to side with Jerry and Tony on this because they are always busting their ass, coming in at about 0200 or 0300 in the morning, and it doesn't seem as if anybody else does anything. So no wonder they are pissed. The thing with Tony and Richard calmed down for the moment, and to blow off steam Tony trashed English's gear. He is not a bad guy, but he doesn't do shit for work, and as a result he has become kind of an easy target. (I felt a little bad about the chair last night because when it came down it bopped English in the head. And that is what caused all the ruckus. Ever the instigator.) This issue is by no means at an end, but I'm staying out of it. I'll let Richard know later that I was the one who threw his chair, make peace, and then leave it alone.

Alarms were going off all the rest of the night, and there was distant, sporadic shooting. Then, just as we were settling into a good sleep at last, two booms rocked the night out of nowhere, instantly sending us up and jumping. They were louder than anything we had heard yet, and I was convinced it was the real thing. As I was jumping around trying to get my pants on, I began hyperventilating. When I realized this, I tried to calm down and get a hold of myself. I guess the suddenness of it all just threw me off balance.

"Relax — hyperventilating is going to get you nowhere," I told myself.

People were running all over. In and out of bunkers, some with full MOPP suits on, some with nothing. There was a lot of confusion, talking over the radios, people asking, "What's going on?" People were expecting gas, HE, you name it. The power of fear and disruption in this situation is unbelievable. Definitely something to remember.

All that madness last night is probably why there was so much tension in the tent this morning. The lack of sleep, the false alarms, (the two booms we'd heard were supposedly sonic booms from two jets racing over to take out a scud launcher that had just popped up), and these shitty drugs we are taking to protect us from the atropine injections. All of this is starting to wear on us a bit I think.

I've been feeling sick as a dog lately with this stuff. Runny nose, apathy in the office, nausea, headache; I wonder if this is some kind of allergic reaction. One kid in S-1 had to be rushed to medical because of the pills. He definitely had an allergic reaction and went unconscious after taking his daily dosage. They brought him over to medical, hooked him up to an IV, and got him back on his feet again.

There are two groups of pills that we are supposed to be taking. One is small, and we take it three times a day. The other is much larger, a "horse pill." We take it two times a day.

I've decided to quit taking the stuff. It is just not worth it. I feel like crap all the time, and my working abilities have been seriously degraded. I'll go cold turkey on the pills and wait for the drug to work its way out of my system. I would rather take my chances with the Iraqis than keep taking this stuff. It seems kind of piss poor that they would wait for the very last minute to employ this stuff. Have they figured in how it affects our performance? Are the grunts having to take this crap? I wonder if it even works, and if it does why we haven't had the chance to get used to it or the chance to identify those people whom it affects adversely.

At another formation today, Colonel Coop told us the two booms we heard last night were the sonic booms of two British jets zooming over toward Iraq. But more than a few people are thinking they were actual scuds that impacted somewhere in the desert, and they are not telling us to keep us calm. Others are saying they were misfired Patriots. Who knows?

20 January 1991

Beautiful day today. The cool, sun-washed smell of summer — easy, free, relaxing. Almost hard to believe we are actually at war. I talked to Maryanne today. She said everybody must have got tired of the twenty-four hour coverage because they have reduced it to spot reporting and periodic updates. Something to remember: the initial excitement of going to war soon wears off. People just can't keep up that steady emotional pitch for too long. It wears them down, and in the come down after the emotional exhaustion, comes resignation and tired acceptance. This is a dangerous point to be in because you won't care as much about whatever is going on. This is as true of the public as it is of the individual soldier.

Last night was very quiet. I was still feeling pretty sick from all the pills, so I left work early, took a shower, ate, and went to bed at about 1830. I woke briefly at 0400 — I had slept like a baby — then went back to sleep until 0630. I woke up the next morning feeling a hundred percent better than I had the night before. It almost seems that everybody was tired last night because there was so little activity overall. No air raid sirens, no scuds, nothing happening. It was the third night of the war; I guess that is time enough for all that nervous energy and bottled adrenalin to finally wear off and for your body to wear down. Everybody probably needed a rest.

Strange how the very scope of this conflict as a world event ties in so many different people to its rhythms and cycles. Because of television and our modern communication abilities, everything is so high speed and happens with such immediacy that the effects of even the smallest event take on global proportion.

21 January 1991

Last night nine scuds were launched, about four or five of which hit. The Patriots took out about two of them. Alarms were going off all night about every two hours. The traffic on the Motorolas was even worse. Major Howard and Tony each have one, and Major Howard keeps his turned up pretty loud because he can't hear that well, so we kept waking up to the different bursts of radio talk all night long.

The talk that we hear on the Motorolas is interesting, to say the least, and underscores the fact that there really is no good defensive control over the air stations and that defensive coordination is really just a pipe dream.

"Whose word was it that set off the alarm?"

"Word came over the gun loop."

"What the hell is the gun loop?"

"Damned if I know — that's above my level."

Then later:

"Did you sound the alarm?"

"I thought your people did."

"I was under the impression that Captain O'Brien initiated the siren."

At the other air stations things are no better. After one scud alert at Al Kibrit, CWO3 Coleman Brady was assigned to head an NBC monitoring team to check out the NBC environment in the local area, despite the fact that he had never done it before and didn't really know how. He used some M-9 tape to do it. "I had some, so I used it. But I didn't know what the hell I was doing. I rubbed it around a bit, it looked good, so I gave the 'all clear.'"

As I've said before, there really is no centralized defensive command for the air stations. There is the MAG that uses the station, but it isn't always tied in with the MWSS or the numerous other organizations that are also part of the air station. The MPs do all the patrolling under the auspices of the MAG, but if anything goes down, units are expected to deal with it on their own and not as part of a concerted effort directed from one central control point. I hope Saddam Hussein doesn't have the military capability to take advantage of this situation. I'm sure we would. Our SEALs and UDTs would have a ball attacking an enemy encampment set up like ours. They would have a field day.

Actually the TV and the radio are the best warning system we have for scud missile attacks. Our sirens are always about fifteen minutes late. If we keep the TV on, we can hear the sirens going off over CNN before we hear our own. It takes time for word to get passed down from higher headquarters that a scud launch has just taken place, while CNN picks up the information right off. So we actually use CNN as our fail-safe alarm system.

Dharan and Jubail Airport were both supposedly hit by scuds last night, but they either landed in the desert or got taken out by Patriot missiles, so they didn't really do any damage. The scuds are becoming almost a joke now. We don't even listen to the alarms anymore; by the time they go off, you know it's all clear because the scuds have already impacted. Instead we all wake up for a moment, crack a few jokes, wait to see if anything serious is going on, then roll over and go back to sleep. So much for the great scud missile barrage that I was expecting.

That cartoon of the Iraqi scud missile launcher, with the scud in the camel's ass and Saddam about to stamp on his gonads to set it off, is closer to the truth. Saddam's whole effort and conduct of this war is almost a joke. Does he have any idea what the hell he is doing? What a loser.

Bad intelligence news today. They are expecting 80% casualties in the engineers during the initial ground assault.

CNN is definitely leaving a legacy behind in its coverage of this war, but sometimes it is taking it all to extremes that border on the comical. All the reporters think they are so intrepid and brave to be getting the story with death and danger all about, but much of the time they just look like idiots. Watching TV a few nights ago while waiting at the airport, we saw some reporter in Tel Aviv giving his story while an air attack was underway. He looked like a doofus. He was talking, listening to the sirens, obviously nervous but trying to act brave. "I think I see something, do you see anything?" Kind of ducking, kind of not.

I was almost wishing he would get blown away right there; it would have put things in perspective for him. I think that everybody might be getting a little sick of the media because of this attitude. Seems as if they are doing all this now just to be cowboys and make a name for themselves.

A lot of civilian panic in Tel Aviv. A three-year-old girl got asphyxiated when her mother tried to put her gas mask on her, and another lady injected herself with atropine. Think of the power of that terror that Saddam is able to wield over these people. We are trained to do this, and still many of people freak out when you start talking about gas and NBC warfare. It's just like swimming or holding your breath under water; you have to relax, or you will defeat yourself. Terror is an unbelievably powerful weapon. Know how to wield it and how to guard against it.

22 January 1991

Busy night last night and busy day today.

Last night I had duty. I was briefed by the XO, picked up the duty radio, briefed my watch standers about mustering points, about being alert, and about reactions to various situations, and then went and played volleyball. The colonel always grabs his team whenever he gets in the mood to play, and yesterday he had the time and felt like blowing off a little steam.

Luckily for us he makes up the rules, so Colonel Staunton, who stands about 6'6", can take down the net when he spikes. We won both games. I went and had a good meal and then went on watch.

Watch was fairly uneventful. Civil defense alarms sounded at about 2200 out in town, but we got word that no scuds were inbound at King Abdul Aziz, and I passed that on to Lieutenant Colonel Staunton. Jerry and Tony were up at the port unloading the Atlantic Freighter, and I spent some time helping them get things back to King Abdul Aziz as they came off the ship. They would talk to me over the Motorola radio from the port, tell me what they needed and what was going on, and I would go relay that information to the 271 drivers waiting out on the lot. The drivers would be sleeping in or on their trucks while they waited, and every once in a while, whenever Jerry and Tony had a full load, we would dispatch them to the port.

It was very late by the time we had everything moved from the port to King Abdul Aziz, and I caught a few zzz's in the director's chair in Colonel Caldwell's office.

Today I went up to IMEF to try and track down two messages that Colonel Caldwell needed. While I was up there, I got saddled with walking through a request for ten refrigerator units that Wing needed. In the desert, "reefer" units, as they are called, are at a premium. Everybody needed them, and everybody wanted them. As fast as they came off the ships at the port, they would be grabbed by the units that needed them, and, naturally, Wing was at the bottom of the priority list. The request needed to go from Wing to IMEF and then over to FSSG. I took it from IMEF over to the FSSG, where they okayed the request and sent me off with an endorsement to the port where I would pick the reefers up.

Everything goes faster when you walk requests through. If you send them through regular channels, the requests get lost, don't get the attention they deserve, or end up taking days to process. If you really need something done, you have to make sure you walk it through. That way you can stay with the paperwork the whole time and make sure that everything gets taken care of properly. It takes a lot of time, mostly spent waiting on different people you have to speak to and waiting for paperwork to get processed, but in the long run it is the most efficient and responsive way of doing things. It also allows you to make contacts, to get things moving, and to figure out generally where to go to get things done.

At the port I met the warrant officer in charge of unloading and maintaining all the containers that came off the ships, including the reefer units, which actually made up about 70% of everything he and his crew worked on. I let him know who I was, tried my best to get in his good graces, and arranged for a time tomorrow that I would come with transportation to get the reefers. You can get all the requests and signed endorsements you want from higher headquarters, but if they don't have what you need at the level where you actually pick it up or they just won't give it to you, you are out of luck.

A lot of stuff is just taken care of at this level. This is where the gunneys, tops, and warrant officers do all their wheeling and dealing. They can get things without going through the channels and get them much faster.

It is also at this level that gear gets stolen. If things aren't properly guarded, hard chargers from any number of units or service branches will grab anything they can get their hands on. Units will often need gear the supply system is just not providing quickly enough, so they either use the buddy system to get what they need or go and appropriate it from wherever they can get it.

The warrant officer at the port was good, and you knew it right off. He was hurting on reefers that were good to go, but he had enough to fill the request. I told him I would be by tomorrow to pick them up, and I went back to King Abdul Aziz to lock on transportation with Colonel Caldwell.

This took up most of the day, but I thought it was productive because I had learned something else I could add to my store of "can-do" information. I know how to get reefers now.

When I got back to King Abdul Aziz, I briefed Colonel Caldwell on the progress on the reefers, and he locked on the transportation to pick them up tomorrow. Then I walked into the office just in time to get a briefing by the information systems management officer, or ISMO, who is usually the computer geek of the unit, on how to send messages from the S-3 at Group up to Wing via the S-1 on the newly established LAN lines.

Had a nice meal tonight. Kind of tired now. Later I'm getting a ride around the base with the MPs. I asked Lisa Dean, the lieutenant in charge of the MP detachment here, to take me out on one of the MP patrols if she ever got a chance, and tonight is the night.

From the Intel clerks: bombing is going very well against arty positions, Republican Guards still dug in and waiting. It will all come down to the ground war, and how well that goes, to determine finally and fully how effective the air war has been.

Feeling pretty good about how I'm doing here. Remember to keep calm and resolute, always maintain your dignity, and always, always, always reassure the troops. Don't express ideas or insecurities to them unless you have the faith and security in the big picture to cancel the other stuff out. Always be positive.

23 January 1991

Good day today, very restful night last night. I was supposed to go out with Lieutenant Dean and the MPs, but I fell asleep and slept until 2305, about two hours after I was supposed to be there. I got up anyway, got dressed, and went over to the MP station, but when I got there she had already done the patrol and gone to bed for the night. The only MPs still up were the ones on duty or out patrolling, which they did in shifts throughout the night and day continuously. So I headed back to the tent and to bed.

It was a quiet, still, and beautifully warm night.

This morning I went up to the port with Jerry Healey to grab the trucks that Colonel Caldwell had requested yesterday for the reefers. We picked up the trucks, then loaded up the reefers that would be going to MWSS-271. We were also able to bring back some break bulk from the Atlantic Freighter offload.

The reefers are supposed to be going north to Tanajib, but since 271 is having so much trouble getting trucks and hanging on to them, this probably won't happen until tomorrow.

Later I played some more volleyball with Colonel Coop, Major Stevenson, and Lieutenant Colonel Staunton. They set up a tournament, and everybody who wanted to participate made up teams and played off until a champion emerged. It was a lot of fun and blew off a lot of steam, and we ended up winning the tournament. Five straight wins after an initial loss; guess it just took time for the old guys to get going. We played some more after this, eventually winning four out of five for the day. The colonel was psyched, of course. Marine Corps colonels are always as competitive as hell in anything they do.

I think if I have flashbacks from this conflict, it is going be about missing the ball on the volleyball court or not getting the spike. I'll wake up in a cold sweat, "Hit the ball, man!" That is about how serious this war is looking right now. Sure ain't like it must have been in Vietnam. Like Hoss said, "Charlie had balls."

Another good meal tonight. I'll try to go out on patrol tonight again with the MPs.

24 January 1991

Took a trip to the port to check on fuel with Staff Sergeant James today. Fuel will move north with MWSS-271 to Tanajib for helo ops in the upcoming assault. I showed him where the FSSG was located, and he went in to make liaison and the arrangements necessary for everything to happen smoothly. For me it was really kind of a boondoggle. Now we are waiting on more commercial trucks to keep getting all required gear north to Tanajib.

I got a letter from my father today, and he basically told me to relax about thinking that everything is all screwed up. He said that things always look that way when you are looking from the bottom up. Which seems true considering just how well we have done so far: getting all this stuff over here in the first place in just six months and prosecuting the war so effectively since then.

What a logistics effort. Think of all the planning and movement that has gone into this, and that is not even talking about the tactical and strategic side of it.

No other news today. Is something cooking?

Ground war looks as if it will come down to a battle over the American psyche. It will be casualties vs. speed. Saddam will try to inflict as many casualties on us as possible, make us requestion our commitment and our drive to get him out of Kuwait, while we will be trying to win fast, real fast, before the American public realizes just how many casualties there are.

Last night I finally got to cruise around the perimeter with the MPs. I also met the other lieutenant who is in charge of the MPs with Lisa. He is an ex-grunt and worked as a 03 rifle platoon commander, weapons platoon commander, and weapons company XO. He is the one who set up the perimeter defensive plan, established the search procedures at the gates, etc. He told me that there are SCAMP listening devices and trip flares surrounding the southern portion of ground beyond the rear area, outside the fence line. The rear area grunt platoon, drawn from a reserve battalion and assigned to protect the rear areas like the airfields, falls under him. They are responsible for ASP security, among other things. He also told me that they had a grunt, him, doing this stuff because of his experience and expertise in rear area security operations and the combat arms. That is the way the MP billet is designed.

He also showed me the interlocking fields of fire set up for positions on the perimeter and how the Seabee mortar positions were worked into the defensive plan. So Jerry and Tony were wrong about that one. The Seabees did know what they were doing and weren't just a bunch of yahoos who were going to get our asses blown off when their mortar fire fell short of where they wanted it.

This sounded good and covered many of the areas I had earlier thought were neglected, but it still leaves many defensive holes a dedicated group of individuals could take advantage of. Driving around the perimeter later, I asked Lisa what would happen if somebody hit the camp and how the MPs would control the response. She said they would control it through the unit whose area was assaulted. But there are no set procedures to do this that I know of, and there haven't been any drills to practice it. If any of the units are hit, we will have no idea what to do, how to get control, or who is coming to back us up. Commandos could sneak in, fire off a few shots, get the whole camp shooting at itself, and then fade off, or use the chaos as a diversion to blow up our planes, fuel bladders, towers, or any other primary targets.

There is simply no single tactical chain of command to tie in all these units defensively, and there should be.

Those stinking pills again. Sergeant McEntire heard today that the corpsmen and doctors are saying we should stop taking them. I don't know if that is because of the reduced threat or because they are dangerous. They have definitely made everyone more aggressive. I've seen personalities change right in front of me with the pills, the effects of which were probably intensified because of the stress of the situation we're in. Sergeant Glenn's been fighting with Sergeant McEntire over nothing, and Major Howard's much more punchy and quick to take offense over minor problems than he ever was before.

The war coverage continues constantly. It's on the TV outside the offices when we go to work. It's on the radio when we eat and in the tent when we sleep. It's in the papers and magazines from home. News of the war completely inundates our lives.

And where did CNN get that theme music? It sounds like a warm-up for the Olympics or something, like NBC's somber theme for the 1988 games. It highlights the fact that all the coverage makes this seem like some kind of sporting event, a fact which almost everybody is remarking upon.

26 January 1991

Missed a day yesterday, so I have a lot of stuff to get down today.

Yesterday I sat around for a few hours in the morning, then went with Jerry to the port to get some trucks. We had requested fifty but had a low priority and expected none. I found out later that it was the Wing embark officer, a captain, who was prioritizing our trucks for us when the requests went to the FSSG. How the hell does he know what priority all these trucks and missions should have? If he has to prioritize the entire Wing, how does he decide who gets precedence among all the different units?

They have also reorganized the motor pool at the port in an effort to get things running more efficiently and to keep tighter rein on the trucks. Previously you went to the motor pool operations center and asked for your trucks. Then if you had priority and trucks were available, a runner was given your mission number, and he went and rounded up the trucks. You filled them with A-drivers, and off you went. If you didn't have priority, you just waited until they got to you.

Now the operations center gets the priorities from the Transportation Support Unit and assigns those missions out to one of the four truck companies located on the lot, right across from the operations center itself. These are A Company, B Company, Truck Company, and Motor Transport Company, who then fulfill the requirement the same way as before — by sending a runner out to round up the trucks and then signing them over to the receiving unit. If one of the companies can't fill the assigned quota, the request goes back to the operations center and is then reassigned to another one of the companies, though they are still all drawing from the same motor pool assets.

Basically they have just added another level of bureaucracy to get through before you get your trucks. Going back through the operations center never works because they refuse to reassign quotas: "They have missions to take care of already with higher priorities than yours." And if your truck company can't help you, you are out of luck as usual.

So, as always, you end up begging, borrowing, or stealing to get what you need. Many times the different companies themselves will help you out if you ask. They might not have your quota, but if they can they will grab the trucks for you anyway. You just send the person in to do the dealing who is best suited to it.

There is also a gunney in the operations center who has the system moving even slower than it normally would, and this makes getting trucks that much harder. He gets a prioritized list every morning and moves down it, filling each quota. Anybody getting trucks that day is supposed to report in by 0600 to get the word on the time their trucks will be available, then report back at that time to pick up the trucks. But he is way too easy about letting people pick them up whenever, so other people waiting there without high priorities don't get them.

Many of the high priority people don't show up on time to find out when their trucks will be available, or don't even show up. At 0700 he'll give them a call, reminding them to report into the operations center. It's only after they haven't showed up by 0800 that he finally drops them from the list. And if they are late picking the trucks up, it's the same deal. He gives them two hours and a call before he moves on to the next unit on the list. If units can't be there on time, what kind of urgency do they have to get things done anyway?

Today we played the game as usual, got nowhere, and resorted to Jerry's usual tricks. We were assigned two trucks without Saudi drivers, so we needed to provide Marine drivers and A-drivers. While we were waiting to take these, I had two more A-drivers jump into two other trucks, with Saudi drivers in them, that were being lined up for use by another unit. Jerry told me how to do all this, and it seemed to be working perfectly. I was nervous about not getting out of there with the two trucks and wanted to get moving. Finally, the Marines' trucks were ready and rolled on out, followed by the two others, who just pulled in behind them. The Arab drivers didn't know what was going on, of course, they just did whatever the A-drivers told them, and our A-drivers knew exactly what was up.

They turned the corner, moving down the street, and nobody even realized it. We were rolling. We had made off with two extra trucks.

Poor motor pool. They were missing about fifty percent of the trucks that they had begun this operation with, and most of them were swiped the same way. The fact is that you get what you need, one way or another. We just need more trucks.

Later I went up to the port again, this time with John Clark and a few drivers, to grab some other trucks coming off the Atlantic Freighter. After five minutes I knew the trucks wouldn't be coming off until tomorrow at least, but it took another hour for Hoss to decide to throw in the towel and come home. We'll just go back tomorrow. Jerry and John had a disagreement over drivers, a lot of tempers, nerves on edge lately.

While at the port, I was shooting the breeze with the troops and I commiserated with them because they were not able to sling their rifles across their backs and they had to combat roll their sleeves, which was all done at the discretion of the first sergeant. Then today the first sergeant said, "Sir, I heard you had a problem with the way I have them slinging their weapons?" Surprised, to say the least, I told him I had probably spoken out of turn. Another example of where you have to be careful about taking away a SNCOs prerogative, or that of any junior leader for that matter. He was trying to do things the way he saw fit, and here I was stepping in where I really shouldn't have been. It didn't matter that the CO didn't have his sleeves combat rolled, or that it was harder working with your rifle over your shoulder. You can't always side with the troops. The first sergeant was doing what he thought best, keeping them ready and prepared for a gas attack, and I had interfered.

Lesson: troops listen to what you say, everything you say. They will repeat things you said because they trust you and because it gives force to their own arguments. Be careful not to undermine the authority of those beneath you. Let them run with their responsibility, even if they are doing things differently than you would yourself. And tread lightly as a staff officer.

Saddam is now dumping oil into the ocean. The desperate acts of a desperate man or something else? What the hell is he up to now? Does he still have any hope of winning this war? Are his soldiers going to martyr themselves? Maybe we should have hit him with everything at once, ground assault and all. A ferocious, unprecedented, and overwhelming blitzkrieg, but then maybe the Iraqis wouldn't have had time to sit and stew in the endless bombings that they are going through now. Maybe they would have fought to the death because it was a fresh idea and a real possibility with death not so up close and personal for days on end and the adrenalin from the assault so high. On the other hand, this long bombing campaign might give Saddam the time he needs to get his troops ready. To restore order and some sense of command and communication before the ground assault does come. Now they have time to get used to the bombing, to get their supply networks going in that environment, and to get ready for the next stage of the war.

If Saddam is dug in as well as intel says he is and the bombing campaign doesn't break his will, then this ground war is going to be bad. We might get our nose bloody, and many good people are going to die. I wonder if it's worth it. I wonder if attacking is the smart thing to do. Maybe it would be better to just keep bombing them into the Stone Age. Better a million dead Iraqis than one dead American soldier.

Control, organization, planning, communication. The key elements, again and again.

I wonder if the Fifth MEB is a diversion? It's sitting off the coast of Kuwait with the Fourth MEB, but it doesn't have nearly the assets. Word is that the stuff on board the ships is pretty near junk. They craned helos on, old gear, halfstrength units, etc.

On the truck question. Is being so short of trucks and trucking assets slowing down our maneuver elements? Or are we short because everything is all going to them? Whatever the case may be, this is something to remember, just how much motor transport we have needed and used over here. It's unbelievable. There are probably things we could trim in all the units, like the frisbees and soft drinks, that would make us lighter and more mobile. But then again we might lose out on the morale side of things. I guess the bottom line is to be careful about the things you require to get the job done because that will become the driving force behind all your efforts.

Talked to my little brother on the phone today. He's still at TBS, and they just went through service selection. Ryan got grunts, and needless to say I'm jealous as hell and also a little afraid for him. That is what he wanted, and I'm happy for him for that, but if things get bad over here he will just be more cannon fodder for them to send into the shit. Already in his class they have upped the number of combat arms billets, and they have begun planning for training that will eventually take place out in the desert at Twenty-Nine Palms before they graduate.

They have also begun training and organizing combat replacement companies that will be sent over if things get bad. Sounds as if they are planning for one hell of a fight. Again I'll bet it is going to come down to a question of time. Can Saddam inflict heavy enough casualties on us fast enough to force a lull in the fighting, or can we fight so fast and furiously that it just won't matter?

27 January 1991

Yesterday was boring. Didn't do much of anything except get caught up with my notes, read, and write a few letters.

Today has been a little better than yesterday. The morning was slow, and I spent it reading, as usual, but in the afternoon I went with Staff Sergeant Lynnwood to Al Mishab to drop off some AM-2 matting.

I don't think Staff Sergeant Lynnwood thinks I'm the most forceful lieutenant because I'm always so laid-back around him. I did learn one things about the Saudi drivers today, though, precisely because of this. Sergeant Lynnwood was riding them hard to go faster. They come with the commercial trucks that we get out of the motor pool at the port, and they actually drive for us, so we control them.

I was being kind of relaxed about the whole trip, and not really worried or concerned about how fast we were going or what the Saudi drivers were up to as they went. I just wanted to let them drive and get everybody there in one piece. But we were not making good progress, and one truck kept lagging behind the others, forcing us to stop about every few miles. Sergeant Lynnwood started getting pissed about this and got tired of pulling off and waiting for the truck to catch up. Maybe we ought to slow down the pace, let the Saudi keep up, even if he is going so slow, I thought.

But Sergeant Lynnwood convinced me they weren't going as fast as he wanted because if they took longer to make the trip they would make more money, as they were paid by the hour. He also told me Captain O'Brien did a good job of getting them moving the day before by threatening to take off with the trucks without them and even pulling his pistol at one point. Sergeant Lynnwood was trying to do the same thing, only without the pistol. Then I tried, but still the one driver who was slowing up the whole convoy refused to go any faster. We could barely understand one another, and the driver kept explaining something to me that I couldn't make out. Then finally one of his buddies translated.

Turns out that of the three trucks in the convoy, the two low boys couldn't go faster then 70 miles per hour. And here I was, ready to dump the guy on the road because he was going so slow.

At Al Mishab we dropped off the matting. Some of the stuff fell off as they were unloading it because they were not the most experienced fork operators. There was a woman Marine working with the forklift operator, directing him, and she was busting her ass. In between loads she'd tell me about the frog rockets they'd get hit with every night, although they had almost always fell short. If the weather was cloudy or bad, it almost guaranteed they would get hit. Tonight is rainy, cloudy, and cold, so I guess the rockets are almost a sure thing.

She said they usually started around 2000; we left at 1900. I was kind of bummed that we would miss it. She said it was cool watching the flashes a few miles down the way. One corpsman has been injured and a Saudi soldier killed in the attacks so far.

On the way back we just cruised, enjoying the silence and the night. Saudi nights are so quiet and the darkness so deep that you can forget there is anything around you. It's just road. We let the trucks go on their own and cruised back at our own pace. It was raining a little bit, and at one point we had to stop and fill up because we were getting low on fuel. Sergeant Lynnwood pulled over under an overpass, and we grabbed the two cans of JP-5 he had in the back of the Blazer. We didn't have a funnel, so Sergeant Lynnwood ripped apart an MRE wrapper and used that. He held the funnel, I poured.

It didn't work too well, though, and I got JP-5 all over his gloves, my boots, and my cammies. It was enough to make it back, though the cab reeked of gas fumes the whole way. You have to watch that stuff; it eats away at your skin and nails and ruins almost anything it soaks into. I didn't know this; Hoss and Staff Sergeant James told me when I got back. So I guess my boots are trashed now. Oh, well, maybe I'll be able to save them if I can get the JP-5 out. I'll take them and scrub them in the shower tonight.

28 January 1991

This morning went by quickly. I did some writing for the colonel, and with my mind focused on that task, the time went by easily. Amazing how good it is to exercise the mind or body, how focused and together it makes you feel. Now the job I'm doing seems okay because I'm doing work and getting things done.

In the afternoon I went off to walk through another reefer unit request. I went to IMEF first and almost lost my mind. It was maddening trying to get this done there. When I walked into the Supply/Food Services section, that loser lieutenant colonel supply officer, who wouldn't let us have the BPA authority, just kept shooting the breeze with this major he was talking to, even though I was standing there, waiting to get some business taken care of.

Nothing infuriates me more than when people take their sweet ass time about helping someone who has come to them to get something done. What the fuck could he be talking about that was so important that he can't take a minute to find out what I need? Instead, I just stand there like an idiot, fuming. This is not good support and not the kind of attitude you should have for that kind of a job.

Then, after waiting, he takes a quick look at my request and tells me that the major for Food Services is whom I need to see, or his assistant, but they are both out and he can't help me. Neither could anyone else in the office or in the Wing G-4 when I went across the way to the Wing's main building. The colonels were all off at a meeting, and nobody else had the authority, or the balls, to endorse the request. I guess the war just kind of comes to a halt for a bit while the colonels are away at their meetings.

I decided to head off to FSSG to see if I could get them to sign off on the request without the endorsement, and I left word asking the major if he could get the endorsement ready when I came back. At FSSG I gave the request to Lieutenant Colonel Kenton, who looked it over and signed it. He is a man who knows what it means to support, a good man to be dealing with. I told him I would get all the paperwork together and have the endorsement for it by the end of the day, which was good enough for him.

Then to the container lot and the Chief Warrant Officer 4 Severson again. Another good man, except he was gone when I got there. Up at IMEF. His people told me there were no reefers available anyway. Nevertheless, I waited for him to get back to see if he could do anything for me. When he got back, he told me to report in with him about every two days and said he would let me know when some more were available.

Then I hooked up with Hoss and headed back to IMEF. He had done pretty well for himself. He had spent the day gathering dunnage up at the port for his AM-2 matting and had about a truck-load full. When I told him about my adventures at IMEF, he told me he knew that scene well. "Been there a hundred times myself, Sean. Some things never change, people like him just don't give a shit. It's like that here, in the rear. Hell, it was like that in Vietnam."

Back at IMEF, still no colonels, still no signed endorsement. Some captain told me that if it was an emergency I would get what I needed, if it wasn't I could wait, and since it wasn't, I would.

29 January 1991

Bored, bored, bored. The same routine every day. This is getting old. I'm thinking about my options in the service, so I'm a little better about being relaxed and just doing what I'm supposed to do and not worrying about being somewhere else, but not that much better.

Lesson: keep goals in mind. They keep your mind focused outward and keep your spirits up. You should always be in a state of going somewhere, but focusing on the day at hand to the best of your abilities. It makes life run more smoothly.

Got letters today from Maryanne, her parents, and Mrs. Garretson. Also checked on the reefers at the port with Gunner Severson and took a trip over to legal with Sergeant McEntire. She has been doing a great deal over here, and she is good to have around, but as with everybody else, there are times we get on each other's nerves. She has been doing a lot of the messages and correspondence, orders, etc., and much of the driving as well. She is also in charge of the troops in the office. She and Sergeant Bose make a pretty good team.

Ground war rumbles. A 3D MAW message on the board today about the ineffectiveness of bombs on the defensive berms. The army camp on the way to Jubail is deserted, and many units around here have moved north from KAANB. There are IMEF staff meetings going on all the time, and a lot of IMEF personnel have already moved forward. CAS requirements are becoming a real issue, and the responsiveness of all air assets is being brought to the attention of many of heavy hitters.

Slow day today. Nothing to do but eat, sit, read, shower, and sleep. Life is moving pretty slow.

31 January 1991

Lots of stuff to report.

Yesterday I spent the morning answering letters, then in the afternoon went to rescue Warrant Officer Peter Hart, who was broken down on the road. We picked up a wrecker from 174, and off we went. Checked the different highways, 4, 4A, 4B, nothing. Turns out the Seabees had already picked him up. They had passed by earlier and towed him in with their own wrecker. Seabees are definitely good to go.

Since we were already out at the turnoff for the port I asked Richard, who had come with me, if he would mind swinging by there on the way home to check on the reefer units. Of course he didn't, and off we went. When I found Gunner Severson at the container lot, he told me he had six reefers ready to go, but everything is on a first-come, first-serve basis, so I had to get the trucks to carry the reefers back to King Abdul Aziz ASAP. He also told me that if I had been there yesterday he could have given me a few others that had come in. Lesson learned: when you need something check on it as frequently as possible, don't just check on it when they tell you. You never know when things will turn up.

I scrambled to get the trucks as quickly as possible. I put in a TSU request, but they had no trucks to give me, and then I had to head off to Wing with Richard to drop off the fuel and water report and let him make a phone call to his wife. While I was there, I called back to Gunney Hendrix and told him to get the trucks locked on. That is one thing you can depend on him for, getting transportation assets. He is a near genius at it. You just don't want to be working against him on it because he will get what he needs one way or the other.

Finally we got back to KAANB. A quick dinner, then over and picked up the trucks Gunney Hendrix had arranged for with 174. We headed back up to the port in time to grab the three reefers that were still there. The other three were already gone. Another convoy had come down from Safaniyah and loaded up with nine. Another six reefers had arrived at the port since I had been there earlier, and already all of them, including the ones I saw, were snatched up by using units, one of which was us.

One of the container techs asked if I could get my hands on any goodies for them, like cammies, watches, etc. I'll have to check on that, it might help out when I go back today and try and get three more of the reefers to fill out the last request. He didn't ask as if he was demanding the stuff or anything, he was just hopeful that we might have something. They are kind of forgotten about just sitting down there the whole time, and maybe I can slide them some sodas or something. No problem there, they deserve it anyway, and it will make them remember us.

We convoyed back after a RTCH loaded the trucks up with the reefers, and then we unloaded them in the lot behind the Group headquarters. We were done around 2200, and I sent everybody off to bed.

Today we have to get a lot of the stuff sitting on that lot north. I need to send the three reefers north and pick up another three whenever they are available.

The last two nights on the news everything we have heard has been about the Iraqi assault on Khafji. Their coverage is starting to sound as it did during Vietnam. They keep saying it wasn't much of an attack and whatever has happened is well under control, but the Iraqis seem to be gaining at every update, and they still hold the town.

First report: Iraqi raid repelled. Situation under control. Massive Iraqi casualties and few American ones, not more than twelve. The Iraqis are on the run or surrendering.

Second report: Situation under control. Still sporadic fighting. Heavy Iraqi casualties. Saudi soldiers are fighting as well.

Third report: Iraqis hold Khafji. Saudi forces, assisted by about 200 Marines, are fighting to regain control of the city. Heavy Iraqi casualties.

Fourth report: (Stormin' Norman) Our bombs are doing devastating damage to Iraqi forces. (What about all the planes in Iran? And all the tanks still out there?)

Remember to take everything you hear with a grain of salt. This might be part of psy-ops, or it might be what America wants to hear. It might be what the news people want to report. Contact reportage at TBS was always like this; each side claiming victory and saying it had killed the greater portion of the enemy forces. Everybody likes to win and no one likes to look bad, so you see things the way you want them to be. Remember seat racing. There are so few people in the world who can actually call it the way it is when they have something at stake in the issue.

Again I'm thinking, is it wise to try and fight Iraq toe to toe? Why are we thinking about fighting linear, World War I–type battles?

This is going to be long and bloody. We are thinking the Iraqis are bedraggled, exhausted, and ready to give up. I don't think so.

Rumor has it some general at Central Command lost his coffee cup, and everybody spent the entire morning looking for it.

Schwarzkopf: "Scud missile launchers are getting taken out, we are almost ready to change tactical targets and the thrust of our air assault."

0915

Lots of Harrier activity. Richard told me he remembers putting more bodies into body bags in Vietnam in a week than were ever announced as casualties.

0945

Sounds as if Saddam has massed his troops on the border and is ready to move. Could he finally be going for it?

2100

Much later. Spent the day cruising up to Tanajib and Al Mishab. Trying to get trucks, of course, from 271 and 273 for the MAG-16 move. No luck, as usual, but I was able to drop off trucks for 374 and 174 on the way. Also Gunney Hendrix got four tractor trailers out of my request for three, even though he only had a priority number of 28.

Khafji has been taken back. I wonder what the hell happened there. I bet that is a story. Two missing army personnel, one male, one female, are also in the news. And Tony heard a rumor that an A-6 took out two LAVs the other day, causing the eleven Marine casualties.

English is still gone. Colonel Caldwell let him take off to go flying a few days back, and nobody has seen him since.

Is there still fighting in Khafji? We heard there still is. John Clark thinks something is going to happen tonight, and those feelings are usually right. Well, we will see.

Tomorrow I have to get more trucks.

*　　*　　*

During the month of January, Marine Wing Support Group 37 sustained an extremely high tempo of operations in support of Operations Desert Shield and Desert Storm. Aviation ground support requirements prior to and following the outbreak of hostilities on 17 January 1991 have come hard and fast. In support of the 3D MAW, MWSG-37 has provided deliberate engineering and construction services, expeditionary airfield services, transportation services, communication support, fuel and water support, materiel handling, and a number of other services. In short, MWSG-37 has provided all aviation ground support requirements necessary for the 3D MAW to fulfill its mission as the air combat element of the Marine Corps.

At Shaikh Isa, King Abdul Aziz Naval Base, Jubail Airport, the port of Jubail, Al Kabrit, Al Mishab, and Tanajib, MWSG-37 has set up facilities and services for the follow-on and supporting elements of the 3D MAW. For the month of January, MWSG-37 pumped a total of 6,330,610 gallons of fuel and 2,079,150 gallons of water and provided transportation, billeting, and food services for over 25,000 Marines and navy personnel.

MWSG-37 also took operational and administrative control of MWSS-271 during this period.

Chapter 3
February

1 February 1991

Went up to Jubail Airport earlier today to deliver trucks and make sure MAG-16's movement north to Tanajib was proceeding smoothly. Needless to say it wasn't, but given what you can expect from any military evolution, it was coming along nicely. Every event we undertake over here seems fraught with such perils of complete disorganization and inactivity that any progress at all, or sign of it, is as much as you can hope for. If things are moving, you are doing okay.

Driving over to Jubail Airport today was cool. I hitched a ride over there in the back of a 5-ton. I was reading a copy of a GQ magazine I'd just found in the trash, when I looked up and realized what a beautiful day it was, gorgeous, bright, and sharp. The truck's carc paint was dull against the hard outline of the dunes that make the highway going to the airport look as if it is out in the middle of the desert and not just five miles from the sea, which it is. Hard to imagine the war still going on.

The MAG-16 move is a bit disorganized, as I said before. The problem is that there is no centralized command and control of it, as usual. Things just seem to be going up there haphazardly.

MAG-16 needs to go north, so you would expect them to have some type of agency like this set up to control the move:

Jubail   Tanajib
Airport   Air Station
          MAG-16 _____ MAG-16
          sending   receiving
MWSS-374   MWSS-271

63

Gear would be laid out and embarked for movement. Gear, equipment, and personnel would be ready at the other end to receive it. And there would be trucks and helos available to do the actual moving itself. MAG-16 is, after all, a helo unit.

Instead, trucks are showing up from all over, with no rhyme or reason about how they are getting there, where they are coming from, or what they are supposed to do when they arrive. Some trucks report in, others don't. It's catch as catch can as far as loading and sending them off is concerned. I found one convoy of seven LVSs that the MAG was waiting for sitting by the side of the road on the way into the airport compound. The A-drivers, drivers, and the corporal in charge were in the PX or making phone calls. They hadn't bothered to check in yet, so MWSS-374, which is trying to coordinate the move, didn't even know they had arrived.

MWSG-37 is getting trucks for MAG-16. MALS is getting them trucks. The MAG itself is working at getting trucks, and Colonel Caldwell is busting his ass to get them civilian TTs from the motor pool at the port. And this is how we are controlling them all.

Even with all the trucks, the move isn't going any faster anyway because there isn't enough loading equipment at either end to keep loading and unloading the trucks at the same pace they come in.

There is also just so much crap to move. Boxes and boxes of stuff that I wonder if people are even looking at. Many times you drag embark boxes from one place to another, and later you find out there is nothing in them but chair frames or something.

Colonel Caldwell sent me up to the airport to check on things and help out wherever I could. I've learned from Jerry that the best thing to do in this situation is to help out where you can, get a feel for what is going on, and be able to brief the colonel on the progress of things and problems when you get back. MWSS-374 is supposed to be running the move from the Jubail end and helping to coordinate things with MAG-16, so basically when I got up there I just sat back and watched them handle it.

In the midst of all this movement, I was amazed to see the MWSS-374 CO with elements of his staff and some of the troops rehearsing for his change of command ceremony. Man, that kind of took me by surprise. I wonder if it's appropriate that they should be concerned with a change of command ceremony in the middle of a war, while their unit is busy conducting an important move north?

I asked Colonel Staunton about this later, and he said that is still the way it is done. You always have a change of command ceremony, despite the circumstances, because it is traditional and important to do so. Still, I wonder if it is something you should spend time on while there are other things that need to get done of greater importance.

As Colonel Staunton says, "Lieutenants; I hate 'em!"

I hitched a ride back from Jubail Airport with Gunner Clark, who showed up to take care of some CFR business. He told me that I MEF had requested nine D-7 bulldozers from us. This meant stuff was beginning to go down up front, and I immediately seized on this as a way to get up there. I was electrified and thought, "This is my ticket."

When we got back to the Scud Bowl, I rushed back to the tent, packed up my stuff, and got ready to take off. Now all I had to do was convince Colonel Caldwell that I would be the best person to send with the dozers when they went off to Division. I thought I might be able to worm my way into position as det OIC.

Not a chance. I barely got the words out of my mouth offering myself as OIC for the dozer detachment when he was already cracking jokes about it to Major Stevenson. "We're gonna send Coughlin here up there to win the war. What d' ya think of that, Stevenson? Gonna take back Kuwait City by himself. Drive them dozers over that fire line." Oh well, won't try that again.

The MWSS-271 load out was going a little better than MAG-16's, but not much. MWSS-271 had been living in a tent compound outside the Scud Bowl since they first came in country. After a long wait, they were finally getting their chance. They were also moving north to Tanajib, where they would be supporting MAG-16.

There seemed to be a whole lot of confusion going on about trucks. I brought in ten reefers on five tractor trailers and dropped them off on the lot from which the 271 movement control center was running the trucks. For some reason the 271 S-3 thought they had ten reefers on ten trucks, and consequently took it for granted that there was still room on each truck to load more gear. When I told them there wasn't room to do that, they had five of the reefers unloaded off the back of the trucks so more gear could be piled on board. This might have been what they needed to do, but they wasted an awful lot of time loading and unloading the reefers that they could have spent on the road making trips.

I'm thinking about everything I've seen today and the effectiveness of the entire support effort. It's easy to get too critical of it all because it is hard to think of all the people, assets, and units involved. Remember the drills we did in the trenches back at MWSS-372; simple movements quickly became complex with so many people involved. And how much more true is this when you start talking about battalions, regiments, divisions, or our own unit levels.

2 February 1991

Delivered a message to Wing this morning for Colonel Caldwell. Then I went over and checked on the progress of the MAG-16/MAG-26 move again with Captain Fields at MWSS-374. Captain Fields is the operations officer at 374, and he is a good guy to work with. He knows what he is doing, and he is conscientious about getting it done. That is the main reason I don't want him to think I'm just poking my face in where it doesn't belong. With him things are moving along as well as can be expected.

In the afternoon I went with Gunney Hendrix to the port. We made arrangements to pick up three reefers and got two trucks to haul them down to the Scud Bowl. Gunney Hendrix got the trucks by telling a compadre that he just needed them for a short while and that he had two A-drivers all ready to go. Then he grabbed Sergeant Lynnwood and Staff Sergeant Janisek and told them they would be A-drivers on the way back to KAANB. He did the right thing, otherwise we would have had to wait until our number came up. We were priority 28, they were on 4, and it was getting late.

While we waited by the reefers at the container compound for the RTCH to appear, I struck up a conversation with the two Saudi drivers. We call them all Saudi drivers, even though most of them are Egyptian, Nigerian, Sudanese, or a host of other nationalities. The Saudis actually seem to be the minority as far as drivers go. One offered me an apple, which I took, while the other was taking the chains he would need to tie down the reefers from out of the storage box under his truck.

I tried asking the one who gave me the apple about the prayers, and what they meant, but he didn't speak English very well, and as I spoke no Arabic, we could barely understand each other. Finally I got him to understand the gist of what I was asking. I made the praying motion and said, "Allah akbar, Allah akbar." Immediately he understood and got very excited. He called his buddy over, who spoke better English, and together they explained the praying to me.

I asked to hear the primary prayer in Arabic. The Egyptian complied and spoke the words that mean "There is no God but Allah, and Mohammed is his prophet." I was thrilled. I was hearing the very same words that Mohammed received from Allah explaining God's laws and the way to salvation, the very breath of God. When you hear an Islamic prayer, it's in the same language that Mohammed heard and spoke.

This is why you really can't translate the *Qur'an* (or *Koran*) into another language and still retain its holiness. The words themselves, their enunciated sound, are what make the *Qur'an* holy; that is why it's chanted every day, day in and day out, throughout the Islamic world. The Moslems are repeating, over and over, the language of Allah, who spoke to Mohammed over 800 years ago.

This is the bedrock of faith for Islam. In Christianity the bedrock of faith is that Christ is the son of God. In Islam it is that the *Qur'an* is in fact the literal breath of Allah. In each case, for either religion, these are the central leaps of faith.

Both men were excited and eager to explain Islam to me and answer my questions the best they could, and they told me about themselves as well. Both men were from Egypt. One, Saud, had a family. He had a wife and two children, a boy and a girl. The other, François, was unmarried. He was a lawyer and planned to travel to the United States very soon. I also asked them about the war and what they thought of everything that was going on, what they thought about Saddam Hussein, about the Americans being in the holy lands, and how they thought the war would go.

They both told me they thought Saddam was crazy. They said America was a very powerful and tolerant country and that Saddam didn't know what he was playing with. They liked Mubarak, loved Nassar, and thought Sadat was good in the beginning, terrible at the end.

Once the RTCH showed up, we loaded up and took off. They both seemed very taken with me at this point and went out of their way to show their good feelings.

When we got down to King Abdul Aziz Naval Base, heavy equipment operators began unloading the trucks right away while I rushed off to the chow hall. It was already dark when I got there, and they were almost done serving for the night. I grabbed two plates of dinner for my two new friends and hurried back to the trucks. They were so grateful for the dinners that I was almost embarrassed that something so simple for me to do would make them so happy. It was late and cold, but the meals were still at least a little warm, and they dug into them eagerly by the side of their trucks, alone in the strange encampment.

So much for getting the trucks back quickly. Gunney Hendrix had told the guy who got them for us that we would only need them for a few hours. It was now almost four hours since we had told him that, and we still had them. So once the RTCH finished unloading the reefers, we told the drivers to mount up and head back. As they climbed into their cabs, put their trucks in gear, and pulled out, I waved goodbye. They waved back and quickly disappeared down the road which would take them out the front gate and to the highway that they would follow to the port.

I went back to the port later to track down the people who keep assigning us such low priorities on the trucks. I was going to make an issue out of it, but before I did Colonel Caldwell told me to let him handle it. I also had Gunney Hendrix drop off two cases of soda with the container guys, Warrant Officer Severson's people, to thank them for all the work they had done for us, which they were psyched about, and then we headed on home.

I briefed the colonel, took a quick shower, and now bed.

Thoughts for the day: where is the Army? I bet they are off in the desert getting a spectacular flanking movement ready. The USMC is the holding force for the Army's attack. The generals have apparently taken their war fighting techniques to heart. In the briefings they have with the press on TV, they refuse to discuss anything having to do with "body counts," and they keep using all the right words, the watchwords of those specializing in maneuver warfare, to describe their goals: "Trying to destroy his capabilities, communications, and lines of supply.... Cut off the head."

All good words, but what happens if things don't go as we are planning?

What if cutting off the head does nothing? What if he just doesn't surrender? Or his men actually martyr themselves as he's saying? I think this war is still a long ways from being over. We will see what these guys are made off when they have their backs against the wall and no way out.

Also talked to Ryan yesterday. Said Dad almost broke down when he told him he had gone infantry. Feeling Maryanne so far away.

3 February 1991

Quiet, steady day today.

I'm spending most of the time on the command chronology. The July through December one for 1990 needs to be finished and January for this year. In peacetime they are due every six months, but in wartime they are due every month. Since I've been named the historical officer for the unit, I have to compile the support squadron reports and work up our own for 3D MAW. A real important contribution to the war effort, but at least it's work.

Not much news on how the war is going, except that Saddam's abilities to do anything are quickly disintegrating under the relentless bombing. Everybody is optimistic that we might be able to end this without a ground war. That would be something: the first time in history air power alone would win a war.

We played volleyball again today. I sprained my ankle playing yesterday, but I can still play if I'm careful about it. I also got a package from Maryanne, full of cookies and also Christmas cards that people had sent. There were a lot of cards, and I read them all, about three times each. It's funny realizing how many people you touch in the world who really care about you, and how times like this really bring that out in people. The cookies were good too, of course.

4 February 1991

Slow morning; still working on the command chronologies. A good volleyball game in the afternoon, dropped off some supply info on some trucks to 174, and called it a day. Got three letters, two from Maryanne, one from Mom.

6 February 1991

Depressed again. Am I actually accomplishing anything over here? I'm lucky I got to come over, but I'm not really doing anything important, just kind of meandering along. Command chronology is going slow. That is probably what is getting me so depressed. I thought it would be done fast, but they keep adding things and making changes to it, so now it seems as if it will never be done. I have to chill out about all this stuff. Like Hoss says, "Just let it happen, you ain't gonna make it go any faster worrying about it."

7 February 1991

Colonel Coop signed off on the December through July command chronology this morning. Work continues on the January one.

Days are just kind of drifting by. As one fades into another, you don't seem to be getting anywhere, time seems to be standing still. I really can't describe how much it feels like this. The war seems as if it has been going on forever.

8 February 1991

Duty tonight, quiet as usual. I've just been relaxing and waiting for something to come up. Also getting caught up with the journal. One funny thing that goes on all the time over here is how much everybody tries to live up to images they have of what it must have been like in Vietnam.

Troops are constantly getting chewed out by their staff NCOs and NCOs for walking around with bandanas on their heads, like Bunny in *Platoon*, and it seems that every outfit or unit I run into has somebody in it with a nickname like Swede or Animal Mother. Everybody, troops and officers, love to look the look, walk the walk, and talk the talk of their heroes in "the 'Nam." Which is where this all comes from. We listen to the same music, write the same shit on our helmets, and talk the same shit that we've heard on the TV, radio, and in the movies for the past fifteen years.

I saw Staff Sergeant Ruggiano again today at lunch. He is thinking that air alone will take care of the Iraqis and that we are not even going to need the ground troops. I hope he is right.

9 February 1991

Another day has drifted past. Both command chronologies are finally done. Did a little leg work for Joe on a M-80 food services sanitation unit that they had at 373. I guess they had some kind of a deal on it with the Seabees a few months ago, and the Seabees ended up walking off with half of it and ditching the other half in a corner somewhere. Now the low guy on the totem pole, who had nothing to do with the original deal, has to take care of it, and Joe is the one who has been tagged to go out and find it.

I called around, and pretty much got the answer I expected to get: "Sorry bud, don't know nothing about it." Since 373 has zero documentation on it, I told Joe they might as well write that baby off. Another piece of gear disappearing into the twilight zone of written-off supply items. Wars are good for one thing at least — cleaning up everybody's supply accounts.

10 February 1991

Pretty good day today. It's Sunday, so we can get pancakes in the morning. The line is always huge, and usually I skip it and get the regular stuff, scrambled eggs and hash browned potatoes — every frigging day since we've been here — but today I decided to go for it. John and I waited in line for the twenty to thirty minutes that it takes to get the pancakes, then sat down and enjoyed them.

Corporal Scott and Captain O'Brien got sent up north, and in the interim I've inherited Captain O'Brien's radio fiasco. I knew this would happen, it does with everything else he is supposed to be taking care of. It happened with the command chronologies, with message traffic, and with the LOIs he was supposed to work up. He is so busy trading uniforms with the Arabs and the British soldiers and sleeping all day that he really never does anything.

Poor English, he really has no idea how to go about anything. He has no sense of mission or organization and just doesn't know what to do when he's given responsibility over something. The radios are a prime example. Colonel Coop got the fiscal people in the rear to authorize the purchase of three hundred Motorola hand-held radios and accessory equipment to take over to Saudi Arabia when the Group and Wing deployed.

Then, when they got over here, they handed them out to anyone they thought needed them. Now I have to come up with a way to track them. English, with the help of the S-4, who bought the things in the first place, should have signed them out with ECR cards when the first hundred Saber IIIs were initially handed out. This wasn't done in all cases across the board, so we have radios out now that nobody has signed for. The ones they did pass out correctly, the second shipment of two hundred Saber IIs, do have ECR cards on them, but English has the cards scattered all over the place. Colonel Coop wants some kind of control over all this, which he wasn't getting with English, so now English has been banished to the northlands and I've been tasked with getting it straightened out.

To be fair to English and the S-4, sometimes the brass can get away with things that the rest of us can't. I don't know how anybody was expected to track this stuff when it gets handed out to anyone who wants it. It's always after the fact that the people want control of stuff and usually after they have already lost control of it. It's the staff's job to anticipate these problems and take care of them before they get out of control. As a staff officer, you have to steer the bosses in the right direction and protect them from their own worst, impatient instincts.

I also think everybody figured the 3D MAW G-6 would be taking control of all the Motorola radios and accessory equipment when we got it over here, and that accountability wouldn't be our problem. But the G-6 wants nothing to do with all this "hand-held crap," and now we have got the ball again.

So John and I spent the afternoon going through English's desk finding ECR cards, which were scattered everywhere, and figuring out what radios we had control of and what ones we didn't. I also had to figure out exactly what it was we bought because nobody can tell me for sure, not even the people in S-4, who are supposed to have put this purchase order together.

It's not hard to organize this stuff, especially with the computers. Today I put together a logbook and a desktop folder with all the ECR cards in it organized by unit. I also designed a spreadsheet and database, which I'll build tomorrow, to keep track of the radios as they get doled out.

Scott and Flynn were fighting with Gunney Hendrix earlier today. Scott and Flynn were "tired from duty"; Hendrix was "sick of their disrespect." I guess they are all just kind of worn down.

One more thing — it's cold out here.

11 February 1991

Cranking on the radios again today. Finished writing up the log, still have to finish the spreadsheets and database, then nail down accountability. I also have to quit making jokes about English. I've definitely taken out my frustrations about this whole mess on him. Even though he does kind of deserve it, and it's good to blow off steam, I should really lay off on him. Hoss is no help though, he will just get me going whenever I try and play it straight. Then it's off to the races on English again.

It's still cold out here.

13 February 1991

Still working on radio accountability. That is almost my whole job now, but at least it keeps me busy. The work is going slow, but progressing.

I have to be careful to relax on all this stuff. If I don't, I'll get so wound up again that I will bring on another migraine. I guess that is why the jokes are so good.

15 February 1991

Spent the day working on radios and bringing buses back from the port. In the morning I was up at MAG-26 with Gunney Davidson and Gunney Ali reprogramming radios. We are to reprogram all three hundred radios because the colonel wants to get every unit in 3D MAW working off the same channels and frequencies and the radios weren't programmed with the right information to do this when they were first passed out. So now we have to go to each unit, get the radios gathered up, and reprogram them according to the new plan. It is also a good way to get all the radios accounted for, which might be why they came up with this whole reprogramming idea to begin with.

The trouble is that the different units never have the radios ready for us. Colonel Coop or Colonel Staunton will tell us to go to a certain unit and reprogram their radios, but when we get there nobody seems to know we were coming and the radios are all still out. Then we can't reprogram any because if we do, we might miss some, and the ones that have been reprogrammed won't be able to communicate with the ones that haven't. Internally, the unit using them wouldn't be able to communicate effectively anymore, which is why we have the hand-helds in the first place.

It is only when Colonel Coop or Colonel Staunton calls his counterpart at the unit we are going to that the radios are actually gathered up and ready for us when we get there. If not, we just end up wasting time.

I've definitely become obsessed with this radio thing over the last few days. Nothing seems to be moving fast enough for me in regards to them. Not the programming, not getting them accounted for, not even how they are being used. Colonel Coop bought them because they are so high speed, but in using them I don't think we have even scratched the surface of what they are capable of yet.

None of us are really trained on any of the equipment. Gunney Ali got the programming job because he is good on the computers, and Gunney Davidson is part of the team because he is the MWSG-37 comm chief. I'm just accounting for it all. We also have repeaters to deal with, mobile units, rechargers, and securenet kits. I don't know what the securenet capabilities of the radios are, but I'm not sure anybody else does either. I've heard from the 3D MAW G-6 that General Moore doesn't even use his radio anymore because it was too easy for him to violate security procedures with it. They said a few times when he was talking over it he gave out some classified information, and since then he has given the radio away to his chief of staff.

Maybe that is why they haven't put up all the repeaters. There is one set up here at King Abdul Aziz, one at Jubail Airport, one in Bahrain, and I have three more sitting in a container outside. I think the plan was to get all of them set up at various stations from Bahrain going north in order to establish a repeater communications net running from Shaikh Isa to Al Mishab. The 3D MAW G-6 also told me this wasn't happening because it would be too easy for the Iraqis to monitor the Motorola traffic, even with their securenet capabilities. But then the Air Force is using them all over the place.

Who the hell knows? All I need to worry about is establishing this paper trail so the CO and XO know where all the radios are.

Right now the written logbook is done, the spreadsheets, the database, and a desktop procedures/turnover folder that has all the ECR cards in it by unit. Major Howard wanted me to sign for all the Motorola equipment MWSG-37 brought over here, but I told him I wanted to see an inventory of it all before I would sign for anything. Of course he has no idea of what exactly we have, nor does anybody else, so I won't be signing for anything in the near future.

After lunch I got sent off to the port to pick up some buses. For drivers I took Sergeant McEntire, Corporal Malone, and Sergeant Davis. Jerry has taught me how to drive a standard since we have been over here, which comes in handy because every civilian vehicle we own now is a standard, and I use these runs as practice. I do my best to get the car moving without making a fool out of myself, but I usually end up doing just that and putting on a show for every-body, especially Sergeant McEntire, who is almost always the one who has to go with me on whatever mission we are supposed to take care of. Today was no different, and I'm even getting a little better at it. I had a blast cruising back and forth in the standard while the buses cruised back behind me. All I had to do was keep the car moving, which isn't that hard once you get it in gear. The turns were a little tricky though. I can imagine what it was like in the buses for Sergeant McEntire and the others.

While I was waiting for the paperwork to go through on the buses, I was sitting up in Major Antczak's office. They were working on the endorsement I needed for them to let the buses go when suddenly the office got quiet and some-body turned the radio up. They announced that Saddam Hussein was ready to concede to all the United Nations resolutions and that he was calling it quits. The war was over, Saddam Hussein was surrendering.

Immediately everybody in the building was in an uproar. All work came to a standstill as people gathered around the radios to hear what was going on. They announced it again: Saddam Hussein had agreed to pull out of Kuwait and abide by all the rest of the United Nations' resolutions. Major Antczak looked at me and told me that if this was actually true, he'd remember me and this moment for the rest of his life. I was psyched. We had done it. Air had kicked ass. For the first time in history, air alone had won a war, and I had been a part of it. While they went back to work on the endorsement, work seemed kind of anticlimactic now, I went downstairs and outside to where my drivers were waiting to tell them the news.

They hadn't heard anything and were just sitting around waiting for me to tell them the buses were ready. I told them that I thought it was over and that they ought to be proud because what they had done for this thing had directly contributed to the success of the air campaign. They were kind of psy-ched, but took it all in stride, like it was no big deal. Turns out that is the way I should of taken it as well.

Now it looks as if Saddam was just blowing smoke, like he has done the whole time over here. He has no intention of pulling out of Kuwait or of abid-ing by any United Nations' resolutions and was probably just stalling for time. The reporters are calling it all "a cruel hoax." But they are the ones who jumped on this in the first place, and it is their fault as much as anyone's that we all thought this was for real. The media in this war never ceases to amaze me. It's almost like they are trying to drive this thing as much as they are trying to report on it. They are shaping events as much as they are being shaped by them. Our press is as much a part of Saddam's "cruel hoax" as he is, and I just hope our generals and PR guys can continue to keep them as much on the sidelines as they have managed to do so far.

Lots more to write and catch up on, but I'm tired and I think I'll just hit the rack.

16 February 1991

Today was a good day. At 0900, Gunney Ali, Gunney Davidson, Sergeant Clise, and I took off for MAG-16 at Tanajib to reprogram radios. Gunney Ali and Gunney Davidson are the guys who actually do the reprogramming, but I'm trying to get them to spread the wealth a bit and teach somebody else how to do it. Sergeant Clise works for Gunney Ali in the MMO shop, so Ali grabbed him as our driver in order to take him along and teach him how to do the reprogramming. We had one of the Hondas, so we would make good time.

We got there about 1000, with Clise driving us up there at about a hundred miles an hour, only to find, as usual, that they had no idea we were coming. They still had to gather up all the radios. So I told them we would hit them on the way back, and we headed over to MWSS-271, which was across from the airfield on the other side of the highway.

MWSS-271 didn't have their radios ready yet either, so we headed up to Al Mishab. We hoped 271 would have their radios ready by the time we were on our way back, and we would do their radios right after MAG-16's.

Al Mishab was deserted. Everybody from 273 was already gone, moved west to Al Khanjar. We were able to reprogram about five radios that some embark people had who were still moving the last few things out, but other than that we didn't accomplish anything. We saw Jerry, reprogrammed his radio, saw Top Riley, Hall, and Scott, said hello, and then decided to head back. They were just finishing up helping 273 run convoys out to the gravel plain and were ready to come home. We told them we would let Colonel Caldwell know that everything was just about done, and we headed out.

I don't think any of them really wanted to come back that badly. Up there they can do as they please, sleep as long as they want, and have some idea of what is was going on. Not at all like it is at the Group headquarters. Their tent up there didn't even look that bad, except that Jerry needed an adaptor to plug in his battery charger. The only thing they really missed was mail.

We drove back toward the port road that led left to the highway. Al Mishab is a port, and something of a royal vacation spot. It looks pretty deserted right now, but if you go toward the water, there is what looks like an estate set back behind a bunch of palm trees. They have a Saudi guard post set up at the end of the road, whether for the estate or the port, I wasn't sure, and at the point where the road hits the highway there is usually a dual American/Saudi checkpoint.

They serve as guides and keep people from going further up the road into Khafji, where the only real fighting of the ground war has taken place so far. Today there wasn't anyone there. Like the rest of Mishab, it seemed that everybody had already packed up and moved west.

We all looked at each other, and I asked them if they wanted to try and make it to Khafji. I was the senior man present, so if we went and anything happened I would be the one at fault, but I still wanted to feel that they really did want to go. Clise was all for it. Gunney Ali just laughed, "Man, you're crazy, sir. But it's your ass. We'll just say you ordered us to go. What the hell." Gunney Davidson looked hard at Gunney Ali, "I better not get my ass shot off." But in the end he bowed to the popular will.

Clise went right instead of left, and we were on our way to Khafji. This was stupid, of course, but finally we had a chance to catch at least a glimpse of what was going on up front. None of us had any idea what to expect. How far forward were our troops? How close were the Iraqi troops? Were there American or British forces in Khafji or just Arab units? I wasn't even sure we would be able to make it up there. I thought we would get stopped at a checkpoint for sure and then made to go back, especially with the Honda Civic. But on we went, making jokes and getting edgy as the miles clicked past on the odometer.

It was quiet as hell on the road, and I don't think we passed more than three vehicles going the other way. We turned off the radio to hear better, and we kept telling Clise to be ready to do a fast U-turn if he had to and get the hell out of there. Clise was even driving under the speed limit and going slower the further north we went.

Khafji was only about seven miles away now, Kuwait about fifty maybe. Hard to imagine, the border just about thirty, forty miles, if that. About the distance from my apartment to Pendleton back home. I didn't think we would run into any trouble, because our forces probably passed through the town long ago, but I just wasn't sure. I kept thinking about those officers in E.B. Sledge's *With the Old Breed* who asked for directions from the grunts and got directed to the front lines, where they were promptly killed. We didn't belong up here, anybody who saw us would probably be pissed off, but hey, what the hell.

Suddenly off to the right I saw dug-in allied tanks. They looked awesome. "Look, tanks!"

Clise jammed on the brakes.

"Where?"

I pointed them out to everybody.

"Jesus Christ, sir, you trying to give us a heart attack?"

We kept on going, with Gunney Ali cracking jokes about the tanks now, "Whoa, dude, tanks!" We had had no problem so far. No checkpoints, no sentries to get past, no nothing. They might not even have been American tanks. They might have been Saudi for all we knew.

Suddenly we came around a wide turn and saw our first guard post. About twenty yards in front of it was a large speed bump. Clise almost launched us over it. We slammed over the bump and then cruised up to the Saudi guard, who just waved us through, even though we almost bottomed out the car right in front of him.

"Good job, Clise! You trying to kill us too? Like the lieutenant?"

As we pulled away from the checkpoint and rounded the bend, the Khafji gates came into view straight ahead of us. They looked just like they did on the TV, and the towers sticking up at the far end of the town looked as if they had come right off the cover of *Time*. We had made it. We made it to Khafji. Now we just had to decide how much further we had to go. As Clise pulled through the gates, the car got real quiet. Ali started snapping pictures, while Clise, Davidson, and I gawked at the smashed-up and shot-up buildings. There were still supposed to be snipers around, so we had our flack jackets on as we kept moving up the main boulevard. The place was entirely deserted. I think we saw one car going the other way, and that was it. We had the entire place to ourselves.

I was having a ball, feeling excited as hell and incredibly stupid at the same time. Stupid because we were so nervous, and the grunts had probably cleared the whole place out already, and stupid for not being nervous enough. I think most of the nerves came from the fact that we really weren't supposed to be there. I was more scared of getting caught by our own guys and lit up than I was of running into the Iraqis.

We went over a causeway, looking left across what looked like mud flats. Should we keep going? We came up to the big ball and tower at the end of the road that was in the news all the time and passed it, going left. We passed the Al Khafji Beach Hotel, which we had to stop and get a quick picture of from the car window. We kept on going. Finally as we were about to turn right, out of the city and toward the Kuwait border, we decided we'd gone far enough. Sergeant Clise spun the car around, and we headed back the same way we had come.

We passed the same buildings, slowed down at the most smashed-up of them to grab a few quick shots with the camera, and kept on going, getting the hell out of there. Suddenly a shot rang out. "What the fuck was that!" Clise had run over a large piece of sheet metal laying in the middle of the road. Not a shot, but it sure sounded like one. I think we took ten years off Gunney Davidson's life on that one.

We cruised past the green city gates and back on toward Mishab and home. Now we were feeling pretty good. Finally we had gotten a chance to push it a little bit and see for ourselves what was happening in all the places we had been reading about. I was psyched and started thinking about what it would take to make it up to Kuwait.

The ride back was pretty uneventful and passed quickly with rehashing the already growing tales of our Khafji adventure. We hit MWSS-271 on the way back and got their radios finished and then went across the street and got MAG-16. Both units had the radios there waiting for us, and Gunney Ali and Gunney Davidson knocked them all out, about sixty total, in about an hour. It's really not that hard when the radios are there waiting for you.

And two and a half hours later, we were back at King Abdul Aziz. I briefed Colonel Staunton and Colonel Coop on our programming progress, which I didn't really think was all that big of a deal, and then I got the word that all the radios were supposed to be done tomorrow. This is an imperative from Colonel Coop himself, and we are supposed to stay up with MAG-16 or MAG-26 at the gravel plain until they are all taken care of.

So tonight I'm packing all the gear I need and getting ready to rock. If we are up at the gravel plain when the ground war kicks off, who knows what will happen. I have a lot of catching up to do on the journal over the last few days. I have notes jotted down everywhere on it, but I've been so busy lately I haven't had the chance. For now this will have to do.

18 February 1991

Yesterday Gunney Ali, Sergeant Clise, and I left early to program the rest of MAG-16's radios and all of MAG-26's radios at the gravel plain. Right off Gunney Hendrix tried to jam us by giving Captain O'Brien the Blazer, which we had already reserved the night before, and telling us to take a HUMMV.

You know Gunney Hendrix is up to something when he is getting people up at the crack of dawn to check out their vehicles. That usually means he has made a deal somewhere along the line, and he doesn't have all the trucks available that he is supposed to have. So he gets the people he needs to take care of up early to get them out of there before the people who are supposed to have the vehicle show up to take it. "Sorry, sir, all the vehicles are gone. I have nothing I can give you." I know of one cook who has been driving our vehicle to the showers, and I just wonder what it is that the cook traded to Gunny Hendrix for one of his vehicles.

Luckily, Gunney Ali got there early enough to hold up the process and send Clise after me so I could get our Blazer back. I arrived, not too happy, and really went at it with Gunney Hendrix. Captain O'Brien got kind of lost in the middle of this, but I was damned if I was giving up that Blazer. That is what Gunney Ali wanted to take out there, that is what we'd reserved, and we had a legitimate mission to take care of. You always wonder if you will be able to stand up to a staff NCO when it comes right down to it, and since I'm not all that forceful of a person, I was doubly unsure of how successful I would be. The worst thing is to be made a fool of as an officer. If you push things, you better get results, or from there on out, your credibility is shot.

This time I just didn't give up, and in the end Gunney Hendrix backed off. He tried to bring in Colonel Caldwell, but I wouldn't let him and we took off before Gunney Hendrix could do anything about it. I was still pretty wound up over the whole thing because we had really gone at it, waking up almost the entire area, and I didn't have a feeling for how I came off. Then Clise managed to put it all in perspective: "I didn't think you had it in you, sir."

As usual Sergeant Clise drove. And, as usual, he drove way above any of the accepted speed limits, which I have to admit I love. It's fun as hell to drive with Clise.

At Tanajib they had the radios ready and waiting for us. We were in and out of there in a flash. Same thing at Al Mishab. We got there, they had the radios ready, we programmed them, and we were gone. Now all we had left to do were the radios that had gone northwest to the gravel plain with MAG-26, MAG-16, and MWSS-273. This meant a long haul over a huge, eight-lane road that ran through the desert to Al Khanjar. Supplies had been flowing along this road night and day for months. You would see the convoys pulling off into the desert just before Al Mishab and then maybe pulling into the chow hall that was located right after the turnoff. They would grab some eats, hit the porta-potty, and then head on down the road.

Eight hours later, if they were lucky and all went well, they would arrive at Al Khanjar, the gravel plain, or Lonesome Dove as it has come to be called. This is the last stop for the Marines and the point at which we will kick off the ground assault into Kuwait. This is where the engineers are, the grunts, maintenance facilities, and all the close-in air assets they will need to begin the assault. Jerry's job at Al Mishab was helping 273 coordinate its move from Al Mishab to Al Khanjar, and like everybody else its convoys just fell in with the huge flow of vehicles that was traveling down that human and vehicular river.

The road itself goes straight through the desert. It is about eight lanes wide, with a good thirty yards between each lane. The four right lanes are for going, the four left lanes for coming, with the lanes in the middle sometimes getting used for either direction. At night it reminded me of driving after a heavy snowstorm back home in New England. You couldn't really see anybody else around, maybe some headlights now and then, but nothing more, and you would just be piling through white sand for hours. I would be drifting in and out of sleep at night, completely disoriented. Thinking for the moment that I was back home and then remembering that we were actually driving through the deserts of Saudi Arabia.

It's easy to lose the track of the road at night. There are just funnels in the road where the other vehicles have gone before, and as when one is driving or skiing in snow, many of the tracks pick up and go on for a bit, then disappear into the sand. So you are going one way, realize that you are getting led off another way, reorient yourself, and do the same thing again about fifteen minutes later. Earlier in the operation it was easier to get out there because there were many more vehicles moving on the road. At all hours there would be convoys cruising to or from Al Khanjar, and it was much harder to lose direction. Now with the ground war coming up much of the movement is done, and there aren't quite as many trucks on the road.

You still pass units just hanging out in the desert, guard posts, M.P. stations, checkpoints, broken-down vehicles, broken-down tanks, amtraks, you name it, it's out there on the road. And everybody is getting ready. If you look right, only about twenty or thirty miles away, that is where the Iraqis are dug in and waiting.

Our trip out to Al Khanjar was out of control. Normally it takes eight hours to get out there. Clise took two and a half. We were flying by convoys, skidding through piles of sand off the side of the road to get around them, and hopping from one lane to the next to get in the fastest flow of traffic. The trucks can only go about twenty to thirty because of the road conditions and safety factors. Clise was going about eighty the whole time.

Every now and then there would be a sign in the road warning of dips up ahead, but Clise was driving too fast for us to have any kind of reaction time. Gunney Ali was hanging on for dear life in the front seat, with his boom box cranking the Saudi disco tapes he had bought in the Saudi vendor's store at KAANB, and he would barely have enough time to yell out, "Clise, dip!" before the Blazer would smash into it, sending us all flying.

Once on a big one Gunney Ali swung the radio into the windshield, smashing his radio and cracking the windshield. "Those damn rocks on that road, man. Bad news." Another time we weren't going fast enough in one lane, so Clise peeled off and hopped into another lane, jumping over a three-foot high berm to get there. I thought for sure we were going to flip over when we landed, but Clise just steered into it and kept right on going.

Of course this is how many of the accidents happen in Saudi Arabia. The roads are probably more dangerous than anywhere else around here, but you got to get your rocks off somehow. I was having a blast and laughing each time Clise did something even crazier than the last. We were in the middle of the desert, could do whatever the fuck we wanted to, and didn't have to answer to a soul if nothing happened to us, so what the hell. This was the only thing I could think of that kind of made up for not being with the grunts.

It was raining when we started getting close to Al Khanjar, and you could even see a thin layer of grass budding through the desert sand on the plain. The grass was nothing to speak of and looked fragile and wispy as hell, but if you looked across it, the immense distance gave it the body and depth that it lacked up close. It reminded me of the English airfields you see in old war photographs, circa 1940, an effect which was even more pronounced when we came up to Al Khanjar and the camp and saw the helos sitting outside on matting or on the light grass.

It was weird, the rain in the desert. I wonder if Saddam's lighting of the oil fields has anything to do with that. I've read that sometimes in the winter months the desert does turn green, if only for a short time, but I thought that was an unusual and seldom-seen occurrence. Right now it doesn't seem special at all. Everywhere I've been up here has plains of green stretching as far as the eye can see in all directions.

We reported to Captain Perecca at the MAG-26 S-4 and then sat down to wait, as always, while they got the radios together. They weren't ready for us, so the programming took hours. The radios trickled in slowly, with Gunney Ali grabbing them as they did come in and hooking them up to his computer, and we made scant progress. You program them in the field by hooking the radios up to a laptop or portable computer. Then you just run through the program on the computer, which enters all the selected frequencies into the radio's internal microprocessor, and in five minutes you've installed everything needed to use up to 120 frequencies on that same number of different channels. More than just a walkie-talkie, the Motorolas that Colonel Coop bought are on the cutting edge of comm capabilities. I can only wonder why we have them and the grunts don't. Right now they are probably packing around those useless PRC-77s, which are usually broken or battery dead.

It's like the grunts not getting the desert cammies out here. We all have them, but the grunts getting ready for the ground assault don't. Most of them don't even have desert boots yet.

By dinner time we still had about ten of the radios to go, so we knocked off and went to chow. Night was falling fast, and it was already getting cold out. We jumped in the chow line, which was already wrapping around the inside of the services compound, and waited. The line was bigger than any we had been in so far, even at KAANB. There must have been units out the ying-yang there, and since chow was all anybody had to look forward to each day, the evening meal was quite an event.

While waiting, you could hear a faint rumbling in the distance. It would go on for about ten to fifteen minutes, then stop for five, then start up again for another ten to fifteen. And it kept up constantly.

"That's the B-52s bombing the Iraqi positions."

I could only wonder how the Iraqis withstood such punishment. If you got high enough, some of the guys said you could even see the flashes on the horizon that the bombs made when they hit the ground. They will either be completely demoralized by all this when the air is done or pissed as hell and ready to fight. I just hope it is the former and not the latter.

After chow we got the last few radios and headed out, and this time the ride back was even wilder than the one out. Nothing but darkness on either side and as far ahead as you could see. The endless sand, the mesmerizing sand trails through the desert, at night it was just like driving in the snow, even more like driving in a blizzard without the snowflakes. It's a wonder that Clise didn't get completely disoriented about which way he was supposed to be going. And all the while listening to that Saudi mix — Sam Cook to a rap beat.

We finally got out of the desert and onto a regular road, which made things even more difficult. I was trying to follow the directions Major Stevenson had given me about going straight south until you hit a regular road and then going east until we came out on the main highway. At night, however, things were confusing, and I couldn't figure out what was a city, a built-up area, or just an intersection with a lot of lights. I saw a sign for Dammam and had Clise head that way.

Turns out I had him turn too early, and we ended up going about an hour out of our way. We went maybe sixty to a hundred extra miles down to and below Dammam and then back along the highway to King Abdul Aziz. Going down to Dammam, it seemed as if we were driving forever, but we finally hit the city outskirts and Gunney Ali and I figured out where we were.

We got in around two in the morning, feeling kind of punch drunk and strung out. After the hum of the road and the tense concentration of driving through the desert, everything seemed so still and quiet. I had a shower, a shave, brushed my teeth, and hit the rack at 0300. You always sleep better if you clean up before you go to bed, so the few minutes you lose doing that are well worth it if you can relax and unwind.

Today I've mainly been working on setting up for tomorrow, which will be spent getting the accounts straight and all the rest of the radios programmed.

My thoughts turn to the gravel plains at night. The low rumble of the far-off bombs. Laughter, talk, engines, the lights coming on and off, generators, the night. A peaceful camp of men and women bedding down for the night after another long day in country, with the war little more than a thought, while just eighteen miles away the Iraqi soldiers are struggling to survive a living hell.

19 February 1991

Still waiting for the ground war to kick off. Will probably try to go north with Tony if and when it does, or a little before, if possible. Today I got signatures for all the radios that we have given over to the 3D MAW HQ, but not without a fight. I got Colonel Coop and Colonel Staunton to have it out with the G-6 Colonel over signing for them, and finally the G-6 guy had to do it. He signed for everything they have, and I grabbed the ECR cards and wouldn't let go of them until we were out of there.

Now all I have to do with the radios is to get messages out to the different units asking them to confirm that they have all the radios they are signed for. This will let them know that we know what they have and keep them honest about accounting for their radios.

Skirmishes have started on the border already. Mostly artillery skirmishes, raids, etc. I wonder if these guys ever imagined they would actually be doing this. All the stuff they have trained for, and now, finally, putting it to the test. Who would have thought seven months ago some artillery battery would be doing a raid on an enemy position and lighting it up? It blows your mind to think of it. I wonder if the ground war is far behind.

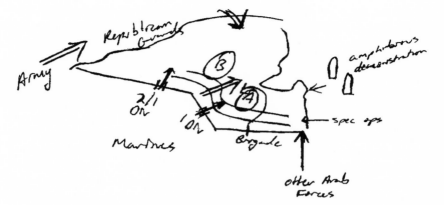

Sketch from the intelligence briefing, which shows the plan of attack.

22 February 1991

Received our intelligence brief tonight on the plan for the prosecution of the war, and everybody was shocked at how blatantly stupid it seemed to be. Even the briefer admitted his surprise that this was the plan, but did his best to brief it thoroughly and convincingly. I made furious mental notes during it so I could get it down later.

The briefer said the Marine forces, the 1st and 2nd Divisions, would breach the obstacles in two places and advance to seize objectives A and B. Another brigade would also attack from the south in LAVs and drive in and back on objective A in case the 1st Division got bogged down. The 2nd Division would pause after its breaching operation, regroup, and advance north to objective B. 1st Division had no such logistical contingency plan and would simply drive on objective A as fast as possible.

The Marine missions are mainly "implied" missions, which means that the Army is doing the main assault and the Marines are to keep the enemy occupied as a diversion. The Army is probably going to flank on the right and Schwarzkopf will want the Marines to keep the Iraqi soldiers pinned down in Kuwait. This could be done in any number of ways, but I'm sure the Marine generals want a piece of the action, so they are going to do a full-fledged frontal assault come hell or high water. Funny with everything we have been taught about modern war that we will be doing it the way the Marine Corps has always done it: straight up the middle.

I wonder if that is because we are the toughest or the stupidest. The movement is supposed to succeed because it will be "quick and violent ... putting the Iraqis on the horns of a dilemma with an amphibious demonstration outside Kuwait City ... and that our forces will react quicker than Saddam Hussein can react."

All the maneuver warfare watchwords again. I just want to know how the Marine Corps commanders are going to practice maneuver warfare if they are just planning to charge straight into the teeth of the Iraqi defenses.

The Special Forces and Operations people will also be doing some demonstrations down in southern Kuwait, and the Arab Coalition Forces will be attacking Kuwait on the northern portions of the main road that we are always using to go to Tanajib, Al Mishab, and Khafji. They are supposed to be a diversionary force as well, but like the Marines they want to do no less then anybody else and are already making plans to go for it as soon as the attack kicks off, with air cover or without it.

It's the air that decides whether an attack is a primary or supporting one. Air assets are limited and highly valuable, and support priority is going to the primary attacks. That means the Army will have almost all the air on call and designated to them, while the Marines will get whatever is left over. The Arab forces get whatever is left after that, which isn't much. These supporting attacks are dangerous because they don't have the air support that the main attacks do. Still, both the Marines and the Arab forces want to go for it. The Arab forces are also the ones slated to do most of the house-to-house fighting in Kuwait City itself once the forces close in there, if there are any still alive to do it.

The attack is supposed to go with ferocious speed and decisiveness, beginning at 0400 on G-Day and having the Marines on their objectives at 1300.

Air is going to be key in the operation, and the air people have done a great job with this idea of lining up planes and aircraft in "stacks" in such a way that the aircraft are immediately on call to any of the forces they are designated to support. All the aircraft rotate in and out of ready postures for missions in a fast, efficient manner, reducing the call time and making the platform available for support fast. One problem they do foresee is that excessive focus on sortie numbers might cause there to be too many aircraft airborne at any one time for the ground people to process and control effectively. This would jam up response time and air traffic control patterns. In this case less might be more.

Again all this makes me wonder if Saddam knows what the hell he is dealing with or at what level this conflict is taking place. Who would think that air traffic control patterns would be absolutely critical to the success of a ground combat operation? And yet they are, and we have people who are expert in it. All our schools, like Top Gun and the Air Force Air Combat School, are unbelievable and produce excellent pilots and control crews. (That makes me wonder if there isn't a connection between the high tech knowledge you need to be a good pilot or even work around planes and the tremendous strides they have made in air combat techniques, which are now being applied to the study of ground combat.) How can Saddam Hussein deal with people like that if he is still pulling out pistols at the table and shooting down the generals who haven't lived up to his expectations? He is little more than a thug, a real gangster, and he is going up against one of the finest and best-trained military forces in the world. Either he is truly inspired or he is an absolute idiot who is going to get his butt kicked.

Our officers are thinking that another problem is going to be target recognition. In all honesty the briefer, who was a pilot, told us that it is almost impossible to tell friend from foe on the battlefield. Our vehicles are supposed to have the orange signal markers on top, which will change to yellow on command. Even then if our troops and the Iraqi troops are mixing it up on the ground, "they're pretty much on their own," according to our briefer. That and the fact that the Marine brigade of LAI forces is attacking objective A at high speed in a southerly direction and you have bad news written all over it. A high probability of mass confusion. The best bet for the Iraqis would be to close with us as quickly as possible and really mix it up, as pirates did in the old days when attacking bigger ships than their own and as a wrestler should do against a boxer.

Again, why are we fighting on Saddam's terms? Why attack him in his own front yard and play in the defensive positions he has constructed? Just as in the Civil War, World War I, etc. We are attacking fixed, entrenched positions with inferior numbers of men.

The smoke from Kuwait's massive oil fires will also obscure things further for the pilots and force them down below 6,000 feet, where they become game for even Iraqi foot soldiers. In the end, our briefer told us, it should turn into a Patton/Montgomery type of race between the Marines and the Army for Kuwait City, or at least it is supposed to.

There are a few other potential problems involving support. One is ammo. (Just think if Saddam had hit the ammo sites, how much more critical this would be than it is even now.) The grunts are so sure this is going off fast they aren't worried about the fact that they have less then five days worth of ammunition to fight with. They also don't seem too worried about having only two divisions of their own with which to face seventeen divisions, with a best estimate of at least 50% casualties among those seventeen, which knocks them down to about eight and a half.

The major also told us that when Division initially began planning the assault they did so in a vacuum and really didn't think much about the Wing assets and FSSG support they would have to help them out. Wing and FSSG had to almost beat down the doors to let them know what they had to offer.

So the prongs are the Army, Marine Corps, and the other coalition forces, and the Army's attack is the point of main effort. I wonder if this whole operation is too complex and too optimistic, or if I'm just a naysayer. The command elements have gotten the word out, which is amply proven by my own knowledge of what is going to happen, and maybe General Schwarzkopf is right about the Iraqis being on the point of collapse. Timing will be everything.

Most of all I'm thinking about Ryan and the other grunts already up there, like Dave, Rick, and D.J. What the hell are they going into?

Today I worked on the messages for radio accountability, the ones we will send off to the Groups that own them to confirm the numbers and serial numbers that they have. Then I drove up north with Corporal Neulight and Clise to deliver a mobile unit and a radio to MAG-16. The desert was heavy and overcast and even greener than a few days ago. We saw some grazing camels and their keepers. It is still strange to see all this green and the grass stalks shooting up in the middle of the desert, but the weather is definitely not the norm for this time of year, which is probably what is causing all this.

Life has been pretty peaceful and quiet over the past few weeks. The brief we received and a few other faint whispers of the impending ground war are all that we have had to remind us that we are fighting a war over here and that it can still get pretty bad. I had another bad migraine last night, dreaming about Motorola radio accountability.

23 February 1991

More waiting today and antsy about what is going on up north. Lots of activity going on in the early evening. There are also clouds of haze and dim smoke moving down from the north.

More talk of peace proposals and ultimatums. Bush seems to really want this one to go to the wall. Also news of more surrenders by Iraqi troops and tank units. Is this true? Or just more propaganda? Many are hopeful about the assault, but others don't know what to expect.

24 February 1991

The ground war began early this morning. It wasn't the same as when the war started. This time we knew because of the planes roaring down the runway. They started very early, maybe three or four in the morning, and it seemed as if every plane on the flight line was taking off and heading for Kuwait. All of a sudden there were planes taking off, one by one, back to back, with no pause or letup for the rest of the night. I drifted in and out of sleep with the roar of the engines as the jets went airborne, but it didn't really hit me until I was fully awake the next morning that the ground war had actually kicked off.

When we got up we heard the news on the radio that the attack had begun. I didn't say much and went on about my business as usual, but way down I had a sort of grim feeling in my gut that it was actually in progress.

I have to watch what I say today. Everybody else is so confident of a quick and easy victory that I'm coming off like an eternal pessimist. I'll just pass it off to my logistics training, where you are taught always to expect the worst, and I will keep my mouth shut.

Now, while I'm sitting in the office at work writing, the planes are coming and going like crazy. Speculation is running wild about what is going on up there because we are almost in an information vacuum. Nobody really knows what is happening, not the news, not the colonels, probably not even the troops on the front line. The news people are going crazy guessing about what they should be reporting on, and you can tell that they don't have anything by the way they present the insignificant things they do have. They are trying to make a story out of any news now. I guess Stormin' Norman is doing an awesome job of keeping the news media and the general public in the dark about what's actually going on.

My own speculation:

1. The Iraqi's still have a lot of equipment and men in Kuwait.

2. They'll fight well, especially now without rigid command and control from up top and in a situation where their backs are completely against the wall.

3. Our forces and leadership have been lulled into a false sense of security because everything in this war has gone our way so far.

4. This is where Saddam might snatch his victory, or at least a stalemate in which he can regroup and consolidate.

5. Or he might prove me wrong if our forces succeed spectacularly, making me eat everything I've been thinking and saying for the past two months, proving that all my negativity has been pretty one-sided.

27 February 1991

Life is still plodding along here, away from the action, away from any sense of real martial accomplishment. We had a party in the tent yesterday after work, with country music, near beer, the works, to celebrate the apparent success of the ground war and to drown our own sorrows about being so far away from it all.

It rained like crazy last night. At about 0200 or 0300 in the morning, heavy drops of rain started beating on the tent, waking us all up. Then they slowly worked themselves into a torrent. We curled more tightly in our sleeping bags, rolled over, made sure we were out of the way of the rain that was working its way through the canvas, and went back to sleep. Then when we woke up today and stepped outside, it was to a fresh, clean, wet spring morning, just like home.

We are hearing the planes taking off all the time now. They go out about every five minutes. Then a lull for a moment and another flight. You can hear the roar as the pilots accelerate down the runway and into the air with their ferocious engines, and then you watch them bank and head off for Kuwait or Iraq. When I hear the roar, I get a sudden surge of fear. I won't be thinking about them taking off, but then I'll hear them pass. The shock of the sound makes the hair on the back of my head stand up. I don't know if it's an unconscious reminder of the scud attacks or the thought of what is going on up there, or what.

The cover title on the latest issue of *Time* we have is "Saddam's Weird

War." Man, is that for sure. I've been wrong about practically everything in this war so far. I thought the Iraqis would at least be able to accomplish something. Now I don't know what to think.

An Iraqi soldier who just got captured in Bermuda shorts said with a Chicago accent, "Where the hell have you guys been?" He was impressed into service when he was home visiting his grandmother. Another guy was wearing a pair of dancing shoes. Seems as if they are all surrendering. Saddam's threats were nothing but empty words.

28 February 1991

Well, as of 0800 this morning the war is over. President Bush called for a cease-fire at 0800 unless Iraqi forces continue to resist.

This war has been unbelievable, and I called it wrong every single step of the way, thinking that the Iraqis would put up a fight. It has turned into a total rout. The last battle was fought yesterday, "a classic tank battle in driving rain," with our side destroying over 200 tanks.

General Schwarzkopf gave his most detailed brief of the war yesterday, and explained the allied battle plan.

The allied plan was simple. Make Saddam think we would attack straight into his planned defenses, cut off his reconnaissance, comm, and command abilities, then flank and wipe out his armies by envelopment.

Keys:
A. Preparation of the battlefield.
1. We got the Iraqi forces positioned. We made it appear our ground attack would go straight at Kuwait and that we would also do an amphibious assault (Operation Imminent Thunder exercises).
2. We killed air, comm, command, and control with air superiority. They couldn't see our forces repositioning themselves and had no way to respond if they did.
3. We kept giving them false alarms such as "Imminent Thunder," and made them think we were preparing an amphibious assault. All this was done to make them think they were ready for us and that we were playing according to their game plan.
4. Then we moved everything west while Saddam couldn't see or prepare for it.
5. The logistics effort was very important. (Made me feel proud that I had contributed something to this whole thing after all. Made me feel proud personally and as a logistician.) General Schwarzkopf really gave us all a tremendously satisfying "atta-boy." He said the logistics effort was an amazing, stupendous, and spectacular feat and that we had moved sixty days worth of supplies into position through endless convoys of trucks driving nonstop for

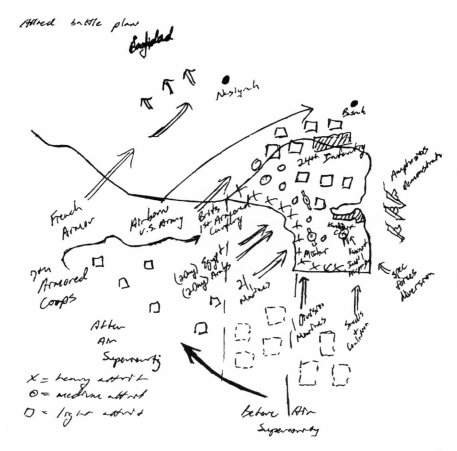

Sketch from General Schwarhopf's briefing shows entire Theater of Operations and designated Allied and Enemy units.

almost a month. (Way to go Gunney Hendrix, Jerry, Sergeant McEntire, Scott, Flynn, Hall, and all the rest of the crews from 174, 271, 273, 373, 374, etc. As well as all those drivers over here from units that didn't even deploy, like 372, and also Sergeant Herman and his boys, etc.)

6. The general also praised the special forces, admitting he wasn't on their side in the beginning but definitely was at the end. They did a lot of ops in Iraq to let the allied forces know exactly what they were up against, both in terms of the terrain and the enemy.

B. The attack.

1. Marines breached in two places, using regimental forces to protect the flanks of the breaches. They drove through with engineers, tanks, light and heavy armored vehicles, and infantry. "Classic, extraordinary breaches, will be

studies for a long time." Marine forces pinned down the Iraqis, made them think we were falling into their trap.

2. The Saudi and other forces did the same, only further east.

3. Then Army armored cavalry attacked across the flank to cut off the Iraqi army from Iraq while French armor covered the Army's left flank from counterattack there.

4. Airborne did vertical assault and seized key areas for the 24th Infantry to take up position and block the fleeing Iraqi army.

5. On the second day Egyptian and other Arab thrusts were made at the breach, still to keep the Iraqis thinking we were attacking them frontally, while armor moved on the Republican Guards.

6. All in all, the attack was overwhelmingly and unbelievably effective. General Schwarzkopf did say that most of this was because the Iraqi soldiers had no will to fight or true belief in the cause they were fighting for. Napoleon's maxim applies: "Moral is to the physical as three is to one." Saddam treated his line soldiers like crap, hardly fed them, left them out there to die, and then expected them to fight and die like martyrs. He was lost in an illusion of his own making.

The air war was also overwhelmingly and unbelievably effective, of course, and key to the success of this whole campaign. The plan was to attrite the front line units the worst, the middle units (regular army) next, and the supporting reserve of Republican Guards last of all. Attrition for each went, respectively, heavy, medium, and light.

The nightmare scenario was for American forces to get caught in the breach and get fired upon by chemical artillery. (Why they didn't use the stuff at any time during the war is a subject of much speculation. Fear of reprisal? Degraded capability?) So these artillery assets became a priority target for our air with orders to wipe them out at all costs.

Another key to all this was our ability to conduct training right up to the very moment that the ground war kicked off. (All of these things might seem relatively minor in the big picture, like conducting training and rehearsals for the troops, but really they are an unbelievably important factors that contribute decisively to the success or failure of a campaign. The same is true in athletics, where a myriad of apparently unimportant details can lead to victory, or resounding defeat if you don't have them working on your side.)

The Iraqis couldn't train, being dug in, and could only wait while the fear and exhaustion of the endless bombing and anticipation of the coming attack took their toll on their ability to fight. (Remember the article in the *Gazette* about the lieutenants and the training they all went through, beginning at OCS, then at TBS and after, getting ready for the assault on Iwo Jima, way before it actually went off. It was very specific to the mission and hard. And Ryan's planned training at Twenty-Nine Palms for this war. Training and rehearsal, walking through the paces, is an absolute key to success in any endeavor, especially ground combat.) We could train and we did.

Now where are the 500,000 Iraqis? Dead? Casualties? Prisoners?

Twenty-nine Iraqi divisions were rendered ineffective. And in the end the success of the air war made the ground war seem almost like an exercise.

It was exhilarating to see how the plan all came together, even though I realized how wrong I had been in my evaluation of the whole thing, right from the get go. It's lucky I wasn't in charge of all this. If I had been, we would probably still be sitting around now waiting for Saddam to get out of Kuwait. My mistake was in not thinking of overwhelming the Iraqi forces completely. I'm too tentative, thinking of fighting as going halfway and forcing your foe to some desired position or indirectly accomplishing what you want accomplished and not destroying him, which is not how a military man should be thinking. "The cut," is everything, and the ultimate defeat of the enemy, "to crush the enemy," is what a military leader should always have as his primary objective.

I don't know if I wasn't thinking in those terms because I just wasn't right on this one or because of my disappointment of not being up front with the grunts and not wanting them to do it or experience it if I couldn't be up there to do it with them. But it's an important lesson I've learned — never lose that killer instinct. No matter what other considerations you have on your mind — personal, professional, operational, logistic, or otherwise — you need that killer instinct to make things work.

There was thunder the other night. Great rolling bursts of it, which made me think of the scud missile attacks.

Yesterday at 1000, Kevin Roberts, Sergeant Clise, and I took off for Kuwait City. I had been planning to go north with Tony ever since the ground war started, but every time I asked him about it he told me to wait. I know Tony was really disappointed about not being up there, but I also think he realized that we really had no business being there and that sneaking off to check it out would be wrong. I realized this after a while because even with all his talk about getting up there, he was always telling me that it wasn't the right time. I began thinking that I would never get up there, no matter what I planned or did.

Then with the ground war going so well, everything began to speed up. Our forces were moving fast through Kuwait and possibly on toward Baghdad. I began thinking that if there was a time to go, this would be it. If I timed it right, we would hit Kuwait as the city was being liberated. So I asked Sergeant Clise and Gunney Ali if they felt like going for it. Clise was ready, but Gunney Ali had to do something for Major Howard when we planned to take off. Sergeant Clise and I decided to go for it anyway.

I locked on a HUMMV for the next day, citing "radio business," thinking that it might be easier to get up there if we went in a tactical vehicle. That night I packed the gear I thought I would need — deuce gear, survival kit, pistol, gas mask, flak jacket, etc. — and tried to figure out from the day's papers and the news where the Allied and Iraqi forces were in relation to each other.

Later I told Kevin we were planning to go to Kuwait today and asked him to go with us. He said he would if he didn't have anything to take care of, and for the first time during the war I went to bed really excited about the next day.

I woke up, had breakfast as usual, walked over to work, and made sure the HUMMV was good to go. I loaded it up with an extra box of MREs and some cans of fuel and made sure Sergeant Clise had his rifle. Then, making sure there was nothing pressing at work, I grabbed Kevin and took his door off to make him more comfortable in the back. Finally we rolled on out of the camp before anyone even had the chance to ask us where we were going. If they did, they got the stock answer: "Radio business up at Tanajib. We'll be back either late tonight or early tomorrow, Top." Only Sergeant McEntire knew our true destination, in case anything went wrong.

Finally we were on the road. The HUMMV was much slower than the Hondas or the Blazer, and we didn't make nearly as good time, but it would get us there and be much less conspicuous up near the border, or so I thought. The only thing we needed now was the orange panel markers to put on top of the vehicle to let the allied pilots know that it wasn't an Iraqi vehicle. We couldn't find any at King Abdul Aziz but hoped they would have them up at Tanajib.

It was cold when we first got going, and there was rain coming on. We didn't drive far before Kevin asked us to pull over and put the door back on. Now we had the cover on, the back flap down, Kevin's side door on, and our front windows zipped up. It stank like diesel, but now at least we were warm.

We gassed up at Tanajib and then went over to the motor pool to find our panel markers. After a little bit of dicking around and going from one place to the other, somebody came through for us, and Sergeant Clise came out with a bunch of orange trash bags. We tied them together and made a T on the top of the truck that went from the hood to the top of the cab, hoping that would be good enough, and cruised on up to Khafji. It rained on and off the whole way up there, but once we hit Khafji it really started pouring.

I don't know how Clise kept driving because I couldn't even see out the windows. The wipers didn't work, and the rain was falling in torrents down the windshield. We fell in behind a convoy of trucks headed north, and I was thinking every minute that we were going to run into the back of the one ahead of us. I couldn't see the red brake lights when they came on, but I guess Clise could, because we made it all right.

As usual Sergeant Clise kept wanting to go faster, and I kept telling him to slow down, especially behind the trucks and in the rain. The rain was pouring into the cab and into the back through the partitions where the cover bolted to the frame of the HUMMV, and we were all getting soaked, especially Kevin. Sergeant Clise managed to put on his poncho, and it at least kept the water off him. I put my flak jacket on to keep warm, while Kevin did his best to close up the leak where the water was coming through. The orange marker kept poking through the partition with the weight of the water, and Kevin had to keep shoving that back through to keep it as visible as possible.

I think the trucks we were behind were some kind of Saudi convoy because they were definitely heading north. So I told Sergeant Clise to stay with them and behind the truck we were following in case we hit any checkpoints or had any trouble at the border. We hoped the guards would think we were with the convoy and let us go right through.

At times the weather would clear and the day would be beautiful, but just as quickly we would hit rain again. The window would dry in these clear spells, but it didn't make it any easier to see through. Clise must have had a hell of a time driving. When we left Jubail, it was a beautiful, bright, and warm day, the kind you get after a hard rain. But on the way north it was sometimes warm, sometimes hot, and sometimes even cold, which it was in Kuwait. The weather was crazy.

We went through Khafji, passing everything we remembered from the last time, and turned right toward the Kuwaiti border at the same point we had turned back before. I was really pumped now and howling at the moon. We were going to make it all the way up there, and maybe we could just keep going as far as we could go. I had Clise's rifle loaded and ready, we had our flak jackets on, and we had the HUMMV. If we were lucky, at the very least we would see the liberation of Kuwait. It might be like the libration of Paris or something else in World War II. I kept saying this like rote, over and over, and Kevin and Sergeant Clise were laughing the whole time at how much I was getting off on it.

Sergeant Clise was having a good time but didn't want to be stupid about it, and Kevin had spent most of the trip up to this point sleeping in the back, wrapped up in everything he could find to cover himself with. At one point Clise stopped short behind one of the trucks in the rain, and Kevin slid down the length of the troop seat he was on and into the back of Clise's seat. He woke up, saying, "What the hell!"

Every mile we went I got more excited and more hopeful that we would make it all the way up there. Then we hit the border. The convoy pulled off to the right, and we had to decide whether to stay with it or jump in the line that was already formed up in front of the concrete border station that took you from Saudi Arabia to Kuwait. The convoy trucks were pulling over and lining up, one behind the other, then parking and shutting down. Their drivers were hopping out and beginning their rest ritual of talking, eating an orange or an apple, fixing tea, or praying, and it didn't look as if they were going anywhere.

We sat for a moment trying to decide what to do and then drifted over into the line that was waiting to go through the border station. This turned out to be a mistake. Fifteen minutes later the drivers hopped back into their cabs, started up their trucks, and passed through the checkpoint and across the border, directed by the sentries who were managing the flow of vehicles through the station. All this while we just sat there.

The vehicles in our line, which were all waiting to get through, were mostly civilian. There were cars, trucks, Land Rovers, you name it. I think we had the only other tactical vehicle around save the Saudi trucks and one MP HUMMV up ahead of us. There were a lot of civilians around, too. Waiting outside their cars, smoking and joking, and they all looked as if they thought they were pretty bad. Like they'd been in the shit, and this was all part of it. And there were some good-looking women hanging around. I quickly realized that this group was the media. Combat journalists, reporters, photographers, and news-people. They were all stuck here with us, waiting to rush up and get a first look at the liberation of Kuwait City.

The only other people I saw in the vehicles were senior staff, majors and lieutenant colonels, all waiting. They might be PAO with all the press here, or they might be joy riding like us. I told Clise to let them in where possible to try and look like we were pretty good guys just doing our job and stuck here like everybody else. But having a HUMMV has its advantages, which I well knew.

"Hey, lieutenant, come this way!"

A lieutenant colonel saw us, pulled us out of line, and got us through the border in a matter of minutes.

"Thanks a lot, sir."

"Sure enough, lieutenant."

We were through and gone, excited to have made it this far.

We had to drive about fifty yards to another checkpoint, which was bombed out, burnt, and shot through, probably from allied planes. Through this and finally into Kuwait. There were two roads ahead of us. The one straight ahead was a shambles and impossible to drive down, but already they had bulldozers working on it and heavy engineering equipment. More signs of our bombing campaign. We followed the signs to the road to the left, left the dirt track that led to it, and proceeded north.

The road itself had long gouges in it which ran straight across it at intervals of about fifty feet. More bombing? Or were these exploded mines that the Iraqis had laid earlier? We would crash over each rut, driving from the left side to the right side to partially avoid them, or would go over the sides that had been filled in a little with sand, but it was still a pretty bumpy ride.

It got better the closer we got to Kuwait. The road smoothed out, and we could pick up speed, but you could still see signs of destruction and devastation everywhere. It wasn't glaring, and it didn't jump out at you, but it was there and testified to the success of our air campaign. Exploded vehicles, armored personnel carriers, bombed-out tanks, and demolished flatbeds, charred and blackened, with their guts twisted into shards, were left abandoned on the road about every mile or so.

They must have already done some cleaning up because it didn't look as bad as some of the pictures from Khafji in *Time* and *Newsweek*. And looking out over the desert from the road as we sped north, we could only imagine how many mines must still be out there. How many positions, how many buried bodies and crashed-in shelters. I wondered if they had even begun on that, or if they had focused on the road. There was also a constant rumbling sound in Kuwait that you could hear everywhere, but I have no idea what it was. Bombs? Fires? Tanks? It just kind of hung there, a dull, steady rumble, and whenever we stopped you couldn't help but hear it.

Then there were the huge billowing clouds of smoke that were pouring into the air from the burning oil fires that were everywhere. It was weird because even with all the fires the day was still as clear as could be. The skies going up to Kuwait were far darker than they were in or just outside of the city itself. The wind must have been blowing all the smoke south or west because it wasn't clouding the city up at all.

The closer and closer we got to Kuwait City the more excited I got. Sergeant Clise and Kevin must have thought I was acting like a little kid or something because I was definitely getting into being where we were. I was also probably coming a little unglued at that point, but what the hell. "You guys must think I'm wacko."

Finally we hit the outskirts of Kuwait City. Now we were cruising past lines of Saudi, Kuwaiti, and Egyptian vehicles and convoys, mostly military. And we were the only Americans in sight. Everybody was shouting, waving flags, flashing the victory sign, hugging each other, and waving to us as we drove by. Carloads of Kuwaiti men and women were driving past hanging out the windows and waving their own flags.

These were the Arab Victory Forces, waiting for word to mount up and drive into the city proper, thus effectively ending the Iraqi occupation, and we were flying down to the front of it, past battalions of trucks, of AAVs, of LAVs, and tanks. This was awesome.

"You're eating this up, aren't you, sir?"

I was waving at everybody, hanging out the window, snapping pictures. This was unbelievable.

Suddenly three American HUMMVs pulled in front of us. They were MPs, and for a minute I wasn't sure if they would pull us over or something. They clearly looked as if they belonged up here more then we did. They each had a sixty mounted in the back with a gunner to man it. We had nothing. But they just kept going and pulled off at another exit, speeding on to wherever it was they were going and whatever it was they needed to do. Who knows, for all we knew they might just be doing the same thing we were.

We kept on going. As the columns of vehicles we passed turned from trucks to AAVs and then to tanks, and as the units switched over from Kuwaiti to Saudi flags, I wondered if we were coming to the head of the whole thing. I know they kept the Kuwaiti forces behind the Saudi forces so the Kuwaiti soldiers wouldn't go wild on the captured Iraqi soldiers, and the heavy guns and hardware would always be up front for a parade, so we must have been coming to the very front. I definitely did not want to cruise up to the front of the entire column of forces and hop right in and end up leading the Arab Victory Forces into Kuwait City, but then again, why not? What if it just sort of happened?

Finally Kevin and Sergeant Clise decided we had gone far enough. I still wanted to keep going, but we had been lucky so far, and there was no need to push it, so I didn't put up much of a fight. At that point it was definitely wiser to play it smart, and I was lucky I had those two there to keep me from overdoing it. I wanted to gas up in the city and maybe keep on going, but they thought it was time to head back and make it home on what we had.

I know I'll always wish we had stayed longer and seen more, but who knows at what point we might have got in over our heads. Kevin and Sergeant Clise played it safe and probably saved my ass by doing so.

So after many of pictures and more waving, we turned around and headed home. It had taken about seven hours to get up there, and we had a long trip ahead of us. I wasn't sure how far we actually got into Kuwait City itself, but I think at the point we turned around we were somewhere on the very outskirts of the city. On one of the beltways heading in. I'll always remember all the soldiers and vehicles parked there along the road, the green Saudi flags, the white, green, and red Kuwaiti and Bahrainian flags, and all the excitement and joy of living and being free.

On the way back, we stopped by some of the tanks and snapped some pictures, then jumped back in before anybody else would drive by. The tanks looked as if they had just been abandoned and then shot up later while they were sitting in the middle of the road. They had a lot of the gear still attached to the sides and in the boxes on the runners over the treads, but we were wary about war trophies because of any unexploded ordnance that might be hanging around.

A little further on we pulled over to gas up and have a little dinner. We got moving again, and a few minutes later Clise got some wild hair up his ass to go four-wheeling. All of a sudden he turned off the side of the road and four-by-foured it in the dirt. I looked at him in horror, my eyes as wide as saucers, while in the back Kevin was thinking the same thing I was.

"Clise! Mines!"

I had visions of us hitting a mine and getting blown sky high, just as in the movies. Then the stillness and the spinning wheel, and one of us groaning in pain with the other two dead beside him. This would not go down well at the Group headquarters.

Clise steered back onto the road, fast. "Jesus, sir."

And thanks to him or God or Allah or whoever it was looking out for us, we didn't set any mines off.

After that we all kind of settled down. Clise just drove on, making our way back to the border and home. On our way we passed all the convoys of cars and Land Rovers that all the journalists, news people, and PAO guys were in going the other way toward Kuwait City. They had just been let through the border, and they were also racing north to get the scoop on the liberation of the city. I guess they waited there almost the entire day and were only now getting through. I can't say this bummed me out much.

We passed through the checkpoint a little after that and then began the long haul back home through the Saudi borderlands, Khafji, and our more familiar haunts like Al Mishab, Manifah Bay, and Tanajib. We got home late, checked in the vehicle, and went off to bed, still buzzed from the whole day. Sergeant Clise must have been exhausted. By the time we got home he had driven about fourteen or so hours, and much of that time was in shitty conditions like the rainstorms. We weren't sure how dangerous things were going to be when we got up there, and even after we got back we weren't sure how dangerous they actually were, but I know just thinking about that took its toll on him as well. He was one tired puppy when he ducked into his tent last night.

Then today we watched the news on the TV outside the S-1 and saw it all over again. The burning oil fires, the burnt-out tanks, the victory celebrations, and everything else, reported by the same journalists and newspeople that we had passed on the way up there yesterday. Somehow word has got around about us going up there, and now all the troops are coming up and asking to go if we do it again.

I wish we could, but right now that probably wouldn't be such a good idea. I'm sure Colonel Caldwell, Colonel Staunton, and Colonel Coop wouldn't be too happy with us doing this kind of stuff. So for now it's back to the regular routine, but if the chance comes up, what the hell.

Done with my notes for today. It has been a long, slow, drifting day. Writing, challenging John on Mah Jongg. I should cruise on out of here about now, but one day of waiting around for the word at this point feels fine. I'm just kind of sapped for energy today, I guess. Which is maybe why I've been depressed all day long as well.

We played volleyball earlier, and everybody seemed as listless as hell. I know I was. Hope this passes. Probably worrying myself sick about not being where I wanted to be during this whole thing. A once in a lifetime opportunity, so quickly passed, and you feel as if you had missed it all. It seemed so easy, so different from what we expected, so disorienting. Now I don't know what to think. Maybe with the war ending the way it did and so quickly, all of our adrenalin and emotional drive is letting off, and what is resulting is this depression that has everybody in the dumps.

Later (2100): Saw Ben Glenn at dinner tonight. He's spent this whole time on a ship waiting to do an amphibious assault that was never going to happen. Only now are they getting off, and he is definitely psyched to be ashore again finally.

It's really, really windy tonight. Tents and cammie netting are blowing around like crazy, and we had to eat downstairs in the gym so our food wouldn't blow away.

Got a funny letter from Maryanne today, which I'm just reading now. I can't wait to see her again. I hope we will be heading home soon. There are lots of rumors about when we are going, but nothing definite. Could be as early as the next few weeks or as late as September.

*   *   *

In the words of General Norman Schwarzkopf, commander of the United Nations Coalition of Forces, the logistics effort for Operation Desert Storm "was absolutely extraordinary … [an] absolutely gigantic accomplishment … literally moving thousands and thousands of tons of fuel, of ammunition, of spare parts, water and food." MWSG-37 was directly involved with this effort, and its accomplishments for the month of February in the transportation of troops, supplies, and equipment in support of 3D MAW were remarkable.

During the month of February, MWSG-37 established 3D MAW elements at Tanajib and Al Khanjar. MAG-16 was moved to Tanajib from Jubail Airport, and MAG-26 was moved to Al Khanjar from Al Mishab and Jubail Airport. MWSG-37 was also responsible for ensuring that these bases were ready for their follow-on units and that flying operations could be conducted efficiently and effectively when the 3D MAW flying elements arrived. To do this, MWSG-37 offloaded, transported, and laid tremendous amounts of AM-2 matting, set up facilities to house and feed personnel, established water and fuel supply points, and set in support elements to fulfill all other 3D MAW ground requirements.

Using organic and external assets, MWSG-37 ran "around the clock" operations to move MAG-16 to Tanajib and MAG-26 to Al Khanjar, as well as MWSS-273 to Al Khanjar in support of MAG-26. At the same time, MWSG-37 directed the establishment of FARP sites at Al Quara'ah, Al Kibrit, and Al Mishab. MWSG-37 also established "hot turn around" facilities at Jubail Airport for F/A-18 aircraft and at Tanajib for AV-8B Harrier aircraft. This allowed for more effective use of the aircraft because it allowed more time on target, faster response time, and increased close air support (CAS) capabilities.

In February, MWSG-37 pumped 12,203,742 gallons of fuel, 2,490,925 gallons of water, and provided transportation, billeting, and food services for over 25,000 Marines and Navy personnel. A total of 1,242 loads, weighing approximately 10,000 tons, were moved a distance of over 400,000 miles. This includes supplies, equipment, and personnel from MAG-16, MAG-26, MWSS-273, and other 3D MAW elements, and AM-2 matting from the commercial ship *Ciudad De Manta*.

MWSG-37 was also instrumental in reestablishing operations at Kuwait

International Airport. Under the direct command of Colonel Robert W. Coop, elements of MWSG-37 arrived at Kuwait International Airport as Kuwait City was being liberated by U.S. Marine Corps ground forces. They immediately began cleaning the airport runways and ramps of all debris, and established refueling services, CFR services, communication support services for air control and radar operations, and all other essential services to get the airport operational.

Chapter 4
March

3 March 1991

Lots of speculation about when we will be leaving. Could be two weeks to six months. I hope it will be sooner rather than later. I talked to my father today on the phone and told him about my disappointment of not having been involved in any type of real combat, or even under fire. As usual he was much more practical about the whole thing and managed to put it in a little better perspective. "That," he said, "is stupid thinking. You should be glad you weren't involved and didn't have to see or suffer through that. All it takes is one stray bullet, and there are a lot worse things that can happen to you than dying."

Still, I'm sure I would have felt differently about what I had done over here if I had seen combat, and I hate telling people I haven't when they ask. Kerry asked me a few days ago if I had been in combat. Telling him no made me feel as if I had let him down or something and that I was less worthy of being called a Marine than those who had. I'm sure Kerry could have cared less, but I cared, and it bothered me.

My big project now is February's command chronology, but I'm definitely having a hard time getting into it.

6 March 1991

Getting behind on the log a bit. Real busy at work writing up the command chronology for February and for December 14-31, which Wing G-3 now says it needs. I'm also updating the spreadsheet and database on the radios to make sure we get a handle on them before everybody begins redeployment back to the United States.

Everybody is getting antsy about going home, but there is still no definite news on that yet. Already they are ripping down the camps and pulling up the bunkers. Tonight I cleaned up and organized my gear. Might as well get a head start on things.

7 March 1991

The time seems to be just flying by now. It's Sunday, pancake day, then Wednesday, laundry day, and then bang, it's Sunday again. I don't know where the weeks are going, but they are going. I just keep looking at the calendar and counting the days as they go by.

I guess part of the reason is that I'm as busy as hell. I worked on the computer basically all day today and finally went off to dinner feeling as if my brain had been burnt out. A meal, then a hot shower, and now I'm feeling great. I really miss physical activity out here. So much of what we do is just sitting around, working on the computer, and writing, especially for me. There is nothing to break it up and get your mind charged again. Just the same thing, day in and day out.

As I said before, it is really hard to keep track of the time. It seems as if the ground war just ended a few days ago, and it has been over for at least a week. I've been tag teaming the command chronologies and the radio accountability programs, and between them I've had my hands full. Finally, though, I'm getting on top of both projects.

Right now all anybody thinks of is going home. Nobody wants to do anything but get out of here. We are all waiting on word of where, when, and how, and nothing is getting done in the meantime. I would like to get going on the stuff we have to do, so when the word does come down we will be ready to go. But that is the way it always is. Usually everybody waits to be told what to do, and by that time you are already way behind. Guess that is my logistics training coming through. I want to start getting ready for embark now because it's going to happen at some point, no matter what. No need to wait for it.

Maybe everyone is just dragging their feet because they are hoping they will get home before they get pressed into cleaning up around here. That way they will get out of it, and the whole process will become somebody else's headache.

I can't wait to see Maryanne. I'm also thinking about crew and writing and basically getting on with my life. Right now everything is on hold. It's amazing to think how one man could have disrupted the lives of so many millions of people around the world. He has literally held the entire world hostage. I hope Saddam gets his just desserts after we are out of here.

I guess I'm tired because I'm repeating the same phrases over and over again. More tomorrow.

8 March 1991

It's Ryan's birthday today. Happy Birthday, Ryan.

I got a lot of work done today, but I have a lot more to do. I'm just too mentally burned out to do it, however. Mental fatigue — when you burn out on writing, working on the computer, or compiling clerical information. Enough for tonight. The rest can wait for tomorrow. I also have to write Maryanne. For the last week or so, I've been too tired at the end of the day to write, so I put it off till the next day. I definitely owe her a few letters.

The weather has been beautiful these last few days, sunny and fresh, and not too warm. They keep telling us it is supposed to get hot as hell, but it hasn't happened yet, and I'm not sure it will with all that smoke in the upper atmosphere.

Maryanne mentioned children in her last letter. Babies! Am I ready for this yet? I've thought about it, but not seriously. Getting married was hard enough. It's hard to imagine being a father and responsible for these little kids crawling all over you. It would be nice, though. I just hope I'm a good father. I think Tony is a good father. He is hard as nails on the outside, but the way he talks about his family, his wife and kids, is very different. You can see it in his eyes and feel it in what he is saying. There are many Marines like that. You think they are so tough, until you see the things that they really care about and how soft they are about them. Which is the way it should be.

10 March 1991

Finally a day where I am caught up on my work and can begin getting caught up on all my notes. Right now I'm waiting for MAG-13 to arrive and turn in all their radios. I have a bad feeling about the turn-in already because I'm sure a bunch of the stuff is going to come up missing.

Today the command chronology is due, and I have to start working on the videotape of MWSG-37 deployed over here. I also have to start planning for the embarkation of all the radios and accessory equipment which goes with them. This means getting them in, properly accounted for, boxed up, and sent home. The sooner I get that finished the sooner I will get out of here.

I still haven't written Maryanne. It has been days since I wrote her last. I have been busy as hell, but that really isn't an excuse. I think about her all the time, but I have to let her know that and make sure she doesn't think I have forgotten about her.

Yesterday we played two on two volleyball. Awesome, awesome, awesome. What a workout. Then we played by teams later on. It felt great to unwind physically after all the writing I've been doing for the last three days. We also played another game of Monopoly last night. Playing all these games is about the only thing we have to keep us occupied and excited. It's probably about the best thing there is to kill time and relax with each other, even though you are not that relaxed in the heat of the game. Pretty intense stuff going on in these games. The ones we play most are Monopoly, Risk, cards, like hearts and spades — I think everybody in the military plays spades — and Pictionary.

Kevin and I keep trying to get the Monopoly games to last longer, and last night we made up new rules to try and get that to happen, but it still didn't work. We go around about three times, buy up property, and then either Tony or Major Howard gets bored, sells or buys into a monopoly, and the game is over thirty minutes later, usually with Tony as the winner. Doesn't say much for Kevin's and my college educations with Tony kicking our ass every night, even when we are making up the rules.

I've been thinking about the command chronologies. When things happen in a combat environment, they seem to happen amorphously. The whole conduct and evolution of a campaign seems to happen in fits and jerks and completely unpredictable patterns. You think nothing is getting done at all. Then later, when you're looking back on it, everything appears so well thought out, organized, and executed.

By explaining it, you fit it into a pattern that it never formed as it happened, so that one thing seems to follow another in a smooth, well-coordinated sequence of events that is entirely untrue to the reality of how it was actually carried out. Is this a real phenomenon? Or just due to the fact that my impressions of the whole thing were from the ground up, where you don't really see the big picture?

A few nights ago, on the 7th, we were awakened very late by what sounded like an explosion. A quickening of the pulse, nerves, the tense expectation, it was weird how quickly it all came back. I can begin to understand a little more about flashbacks now, of a much more serious sort, and what it must feel like to hear something that reminds you of real combat, like in Vietnam, Korea, or World War I and II.

But other tensions of the war, buried ones that I didn't even know we had until the war ended, a sort of subconscious edginess — all that is disappearing fast. Each day is so beautiful. I still can't believe the war ended so easily and successfully. Seems as if the rest of our lives now will be just one happy dream.

I talked to Dave Morrisey a few days ago. He is in 3/1, a rifle platoon leader, and he just got off the ships they were on. They were the ones ready and waiting to do the amphibious assault. Rick Anderson is Dave's XO, and the two of them spent almost the entire battle trying to catch up with the forward elements of the assault force. It was raining the day I saw him. Ryan Straus, the MAG-13 supply officer, gave me a call around noontime to tell me that his brother had come up and Dave was with him. Kerry Straus is an air liaison officer with the grunts who is stationed in Dave's unit, and the two of them decided to come up and find Kerry from down where they're staying at Ras Al Gar, which is only about fifteen minutes down the road.

The last I heard about Dave was from Maryanne, who knows his wife Dale. She told him to look me up if he got the chance and where I was at, but I doubt he ever thought he would be able to. And now here he was. I met them in Ryan's tent and right off pumped him for info on what the ground assault was like.

Dave told me things happened so fast that they actually didn't do much at all. They were all disappointed about what they did do because they spent almost the entire time trying to catch up with the assault and waiting on helos that never showed up. They were on the ships the whole time and preparing for the amphibious assault, which they were told was definitely going to happen. They found out at the last minute it was only a diversion and that they would not be doing an amphibious assault. Then they waited on word if they would be involved in the ground assault at all.

They got off the ships the second day of the conflict and were brought up to Lonesome Dove, where the battalion was supposed to board helicopters and fly into a forward battle position. But the movement didn't go off as smoothly as it was planned, and the entire battalion ended up scattered all over the place. They flew out one half of the battalion, while Dave and his guys waited to go after them. They sat on the runway in the rain for about three hours before they found out nobody was coming back for them. (I guess Rick was with the battalion CO in the first move.) Just as they were getting ready to call it quits waiting there, the helos showed up.

Somebody from the helo detachment told Dave that the MPs were expecting him and his men and that they would be doing prisoner escort for captured Iraqi soldiers. So they loaded up and took off. Dave said it was pretty wild flying over the battlefield and looking down on all the fires and destroyed Iraqi positions, but they didn't see much else that was exciting. The helos landed them in one spot, decided it wasn't the right one, took off again, and landed them somewhere else. Neither the pilots nor Dave had a real idea of where they were going or where they were supposed to be.

All in all Dave sounded pretty disappointed with the whole thing. He is a real hard charger, and I know he was loving life being a platoon commander and heading into combat. I think he was pretty disappointed about playing such a small part in the operation, but then aren't we all. Besides that, he had to spend the rest of his time over here on the ship and didn't see much of anything during the air war. I thought he might have participated in the taking of that island off the coast of Kuwait, but he told me that never happened. Our brass just told the media that to get Saddam to shell his own troops, and it worked. I guess Saddam fell for it, like all the rest of us, and bombed the shit out of his own men. Too bad, buddy.

At one point on the ground, Dave's guys did light up what they thought was an Iraqi patrol with illumination, but that was really the only enemy contact they had that he could think of.

11 March 1991

Started the day with Lieutenant Colonel Staunton and Major Bacall at Wing. I was trying to get back MAG-26's radios, but they didn't have any to give me. So while Colonel Staunton and Major Bacall took care of their business, I sat in the Land Rover and finally wrote Maryanne the letter I owe her.

Colonel Caldwell told me earlier today that I'll be going up to Lonesome Dove again soon to run convoys and help move MWSS-273 back home. I'm still waiting on word of when I'm going, though I can't really say I'm all that excited about heading up there again. I thought with the radios and all Colonel Coop would want me down here, but I guess not. You get used to a place and moving for a week or two gets to be a pain. Oh well, might as well just go with it. I might even enjoy myself up there. The other units are almost all moved out, and they are starting to pack up whatever is left. Maybe it will be a nice break being up there on my own, away from it all down here.

We played volleyball and had a little picnic this afternoon, which moved the day along nicely.

12 March 1991

The weeks are flying by now. No sense of personal accomplishment any longer or excitement over the mission. Just doing stuff. An existence like this would be heartbreaking. Nothing to look forward to, no goals, no dreams, just living day to day.

Waiting for word on what is going to happen with the MPS backload. There are meetings all the time at Group headquarters about redeployment out of here, but before they can decide anything higher headquarters has to come down and say how it wants MPS done. A great deal of the gear we have is from the MPS ships and getting it ready to load up again is going to be the big job that decides when we are getting out of here.

A big consideration for the Group is getting banding material for all the AM-2 matting we have used, especially up at Al Khanjar. To transport and load the matting, which is a DOD item of high value, it needs to be banded up in bundles. But there is hardly any banding available to do this, and I don't think IMEF is aware of how high a priority this is.

Finally left for Lonesome Dove to relieve Peter Hart in the running of the AM-2 matting convoys. No brief, no instructions, Colonel Caldwell said to just get up there. So I hopped a ride in Staff Sergeant James's convoy and cruised up there. He was the one who told me what I needed to do: "Make sure the drivers are fed, billeted, and generally taken care of."

"But isn't that MWSS-273's job?"

"Yea, you're just checkin' on them."

Oh, well. Sounds usual enough.

13 March 1991

Well, I'm up here. I let Gunney Hendrix run the convoy ops and 273 do their job of supporting him. I've spent most of today waiting out a sandstorm, which wasn't that bad in the grassy areas, but really bad everywhere else. Colonel Caldwell finally sent me up here yesterday to be the MWSG-37 Movement Control Center representative. I'm not really sure what that entails, but it's probably to keep an eye on things for him and have somebody up here who can tell him what is going on. Captain Daley from MWSS-273 is really running the show, and should be, since his support squadron is responsible for this airfield, so actually I have very little to do. He is good, and I don't want to step on anybody's toes if I can avoid it. We do enough micromanaging at the Group as it is. As usual, I'll just let things run and help out wherever I can.

Talked quite a bit with Major Osborn, Captain Daley and Gunner Gilroy about MWSG-37, this convoy operation, and a bunch of other stuff. As usual I probably said more than I should have about my own feelings and opinions on how we did things. Hoss would have been bummed and kicking me for violating all his advice on keeping things to myself, which I can never seem to do, but they were good people, and I wanted to hear what they thought about how we did business.

I didn't have any kind of brief on what I'm supposed to be doing up here. When we were driving into the compound, we passed Peter Hart and Coleman on the way out, and Peter is the one I'm supposed to be relieving. Peter waved as they were going by, which will probably be the extent of my turnover. I guess I'll just do whatever I think. One thing Coleman did tell me back at King Abdul Aziz, when I was getting ready to come up here, is to make sure the drivers are properly taken care of and have a place to sleep and some good chow. Besides that, he said, it's pretty much of a boondoggle.

The ride up yesterday was pretty scary. A long, slow ride, with Staff Sergeant James doing all he could do to keep the trucks moving and accounted for. We lost one and still haven't found it. I don't know if they broke down and are still sitting out there, or if they turned off on a wrong track and got bogged down in the sand, or if they just bagged it completely and took off for home. The truck that is missing is the same truck that Staff Sergeant James was having trouble with before we even took off. They told him they couldn't make it, then changed their minds and told him they could when he said he would send them up in a different vehicle or as A-drivers.

We told Captain Daley and the major about it as soon as we got up here, and they have told all the rest of the trucks going south this morning to be on the lookout for the missing one. If they are out there on the road, somebody will find them because there is nowhere you can go on that road where trucks aren't passing all the time.

I rode up with a lance corporal. He was glad for the company, and we talked quite a bit the whole way up. He is a skateboarder from around Santa Barbara and pretty much of a typical California kid. He was good-natured, happy, very tired, and couldn't wait to go home.

The ride itself was out of control. How these guys do it day in and day out is beyond me. There are no seatbelts in the vehicles. The drivers are living out of their cabs, which are packed full with MRE wrappers, their gear and weapon, and all this other shit, and they're driving through dust constantly. It gets in their eyes, nose, and throats, coats their bodies, and completely covers them after only a few hours on the road, and they are driving for days at a time. And the roads they have to drive on are even more of a problem. There is nothing to break up the monotony of the desert. The roads themselves are jammed with speeding and exhausted drivers, and half the time you can barely see with all the dust that the different vehicles and convoys are kicking up. It's a miracle there aren't more accidents.

We also had a tire go flat on one of the trucks going up. I got out and watched and took a few pictures while these guys changed a tire in the middle of the desert. It was the middle of the night, pitch black, and they just went to it as if it was the most normal thing in the world to be changing tires in the middle of the desert in Saudi Arabia. So besides the dust, they ended up covered in grease, oil, and gas. They have to be able to change tires, know a little about fixing transmissions and engines, and basically do whatever else it takes to keep their vehicles on the road. They literally live out of their trucks, going days without a shower; nobody can ever tell me these guys and gals didn't bust their ass. They have probably worked harder than anybody in this whole damn war.

We got in late, had some hot chow they had waiting for us, chili and beans or something like that, with bread, and man did that taste good. Then we bedded down for the night. Most of the drivers slept in their cabs, but one guy wanted to sleep in the tents. I followed Captain Daley to our own tent, where I ended up sleeping on a piece of plywood because it was too dark to find the extra cots and I was too lazy to figure out where they were. The plywood was at an angle, so I kept sliding down it into the rocks that lay at the end of it, but I was too tired to care much. I just wanted to sleep.

Today I PT'd for the first time in a long while. I ran with Captain Daley and the major, and we had a pretty good little run out of the camp, down one of the roads leading into the desert, and then back. After toweling off and putting on some clean clothes, I felt like a new man. Clean and completely refreshed.

Al Khanjar — Lonesome Dove — the gravel plain. Only a few weeks ago this was home to Division, FSSG, and Wing units all getting ready for the ground assault. The entire camp covered a huge area and was subdivided into a whole bunch of living and working compounds where the different units did what they needed to do to prepare for the assault. The place is almost empty now. About the only thing left on the Wing side are the piles of banded AM-2 matting laying in three big groups outside our compound. That and the ASP are really all that MWSS-273 has to move, then they get out of here.

There are other units still around in some of the other compounds, like

Maintenance Battalion and some FSSG units, but besides them and 273 the place is cleared out. You can walk around in the deserted camp areas where the different units used to be and get a good idea of how things were laid out. The berms and sand piles are still standing that protected the areas where the tents and equipment used to be from arty or air attack, and if you keep going through them, you will go right out of the camp and into the open desert.

The desert is strange. There is no noise except the wind, and that seems to be blowing constantly. Then if you open your mouth, it kind of sucks your breath away, that and the dry heat. Distances don't seem like anything. You'll see a rock a little ways away, decide to go and check it out, and end up walking two or three times as far as you anticipated. And all this happens on a clear day. The rest of the time it's blowing sand, and you can't see anything. So you just stay in the tent and relax. Sleep, read, write, and wait for the early evening when the wind dies.

There is still grass in the desert, and out in the desert where it grows, the wind doesn't pick up any of the sand. If you leave the compound, which is all sand because of the coming and going of the vehicles and the camps and people, you can get out of the sandstorm. But in the compound you would never know that. The first few days we were completely whited in every day from morning till early evening.

Every now and then you come across gear that was left behind in the abandoned compounds, but most of it is junk. I know some of the pack rats who are still up here already went through it and took anything they could use. When Captain Daley went through it, he said he found a few light fixtures that he has plugged in at our tent right now. I found batteries, some discarded pots and pans, wood, and a bunch of other junk, but nothing good. It's kind of neat being up here, seeing the last of Lonesome Dove packed up and carted off. Soon there will be nothing left of this place except drifting sand and trashed gear.

We are running into the ground the trucks we are using to haul the gear we have left. Today we had two civilian trucks and two 5-tons go down, and we had one from last night. Bad transfer cases, hydraulic hoses, etc. Captain Daley is a motor transport officer by trade. He keeps telling me that if the war had gone on any longer and we had kept treating the vehicles as we had been, all of our transportation assets would have been out of commission in weeks.

Gunney Hendrix has the trucks coming and going on their own, which isn't a bad thing if it is done right. He spends his time scouring the countryside for other broken-down vehicles from which he can steal parts to keep up our trucks. Sometimes he even steals whole vehicles. Then he has the drivers who know a little about engines repair the broken trucks and keep them running. But there is no real organization to any of this. He has no idea where trucks are from one moment to the next. There are drivers and trucks coming and going at all hours, and he is bossing them around and switching the rules on them all the time for no apparent reason that they can see.

Then he has pissed off Captain Daley and the major because he is fighting with them over how to use the vehicles. I guess Colonel Caldwell told him to only move the matting, so that is all he is doing, and all he is letting be done by the drivers and vehicles of the other support squadrons in the Group, who were sent up here to help out. But Captain Daley and the major have their own agenda and were under the impression that they were running the entire operation, including getting the matting moved. Both sides are right, and the problem, as usual, is that Group is trying to do more than it should to make things happen in its subordinate units. We just don't seem to let the support squadrons run anything on their own. They have to get the ASP moved and the matting, and there just aren't enough assets to get it all done as quickly as everybody wants.

So Colonel Caldwell sent Gunney Hendrix out to get as many trucks as he could find or steal and then use them to move the AM-2 matting to Al Mishab as fast as possible. And he keeps sending up other vehicles and convoys from the other support squadrons, who are tasked to help out 273. Gunney Hendrix is doing this to the best of his ability, and he is scrounging his ass off and keeping this whole thing going with band-aids and chicken wire, but he probably wouldn't have to do that if the move was really, truly organized and planned out in the first place.

It's ironic, but for every truck Hendrix scrounges parts for and gets up, or every truck he steals, he probably could have kept three or four from going down by just following regular maintenance procedures.

What Captain Daley does need are straps and chains. Maybe we can help him with that.

Sitting around today in the tent. The weather is warm, the wind is blowing hard outside, and sand and dust are all you can see if you duck your head out. The flaps of the tent are beating back and forth. Dust is everywhere, coating anything that isn't covered. Sleeping all day on the cot with the sleeping bag under your head, just taking it easy, in and out of sleep listening to the captain and the major talk about seafood and steak back home, and where the best places to get crabs are in Beaufort. Listening to the radio for any word of the returning trucks. Maybe getting up later, having a walk around. Eating the dried pears or peaches out of the MREs. And going over to chow in the early evening.

Life is pretty good up here. You can take it easy, catch up on your thinking, and watch the load out taking place. If it keeps up the way it is going, we should be done in about a week.

Wonder what they will do with the MPS backload. I hope they will stage all the stuff in one area and bring in a special team to get it ready and loaded back up. Let everybody else head home. If that happens, maybe we will be out of here by the end of the month.

14 March 1991

Another relaxing day. Spent the morning walking through the deserted camps and outside the perimeter of the compound. It was very quiet outside the compound in the desert, which was covered with a layer of grass even this late in the season because of all the rain and strange weather that resulted from the clouds of soot and smoke coming from the oil fires up north, quiet except for the wind. The wind blew constantly. If you opened your mouth, it made a strange roaring sound going through it and seemed to suck your breath away. So you closed it, and again everything was quiet.

In the tent Captain Daley, Major Osborn, and Gunner Gilroy talked about building houses and East Coast food, especially seafood. I slept and read while they talked, but I could still hear them getting excited about salmon steaks and prime rib. If they were from California, they would be talking about Mexican food.

All in all it was a calm, quiet, warm day when you had nothing to do but laze around. It reminded me of the beach op we did back at MWSS-372, when Eddie and I passed the time eating Teddy Grahams in the tent, which was right on the beach, while they drove the equipment on and off the LCUs in front of us. Or of waiting at the Naval Academy in the summertime until your cruise kicked off.

Later Major Osborn had me recon a new route for the convoys with Lance Corporal Pollock.

15 March 1991

Yesterday quiet and uneventful until just before dinner, when Major Osborn sent me and a driver out to recon a new route for the trucks to use getting up here. Lance Corporal Pollock from Indiana was the driver, a good kid and fun to be with. Right away he asked how many years I had been in the Marine Corps. I told him four in May.

"No way, sir! You look a lot younger, I never would have thought you had been in for four years." I don't know if this is good or bad.

Lance Corporal Pollock is the one who found this new route in the first place. It goes straight north at the point where the normal road goes west, and he thought it might be better because it was less traveled and harder, so you could go faster. Major Osborn wanted me to check it out with the lance corporal and mark it so the drivers could start using it.

We cruised down the road, which was paved for quite a ways going east, marking the turns and the route as we went. There was a lot of unexploded 155 ammo standing up by the side of the road and a lot of other gear like boxes of boots or trousers that had fallen off trucks or been left behind. At one turn we would put one stake in, at another we would have to put in several. We tied white cloth to each stake, then spray painted the stakes and any other debris we could find lying around to make sure each turn was clearly and obviously marked. The lance corporal was adamant about this and kept at every marker until he was satisfied with it.

We stopped a little further on to pick up some abandoned pallets for arrow signs we had put in back near Al Khanjar, and then we went on until we hit the Al Mishab road to go right and home. On the way back to Al Khanjar from the Al Mishab road, I told Lance Corporal Pollock to take a mileage reading so we would have something to compare with the miles we had driven out. Which route was shorter would be the deciding factor on which one we used.

We hit the Al Mishab road and turned right. About ten miles down the road we turned right again for Al Khanjar, which was twenty-five more miles from the road junction. We went about five miles, and then a tire blew. Pollock pulled over. The tire was completely shot. The road was out in the middle of nowhere, but it was no big deal being stranded there because there were convoys passing all the time.

I told Pollock to hop the next one and head back to camp to grab a spare tire or a wrecker or whatever he needed to come back and get me and the vehicle home. In the meantime I'd wait in the truck to make sure no Gunney Hendrix walked off with it or used it for a parts factory. It was dark, and trucks were passing about every ten minutes, so it didn't take Pollock long to catch a ride. He flagged the next convoy down, hopped in, and took off. The trucks pulled out, their engines running hard through the gears and belching exhaust, and in about five minutes they were gone. Out of sight and sound down the road, and the desert was quiet again.

The Marines in every convoy that went by would stop and ask if I needed help. I was fine, and I told them so. I even enjoyed being out there by myself, so I was almost disappointed when I could see the lights of another convoy coming toward me in the distance. When they stopped, I would tell them that I was waiting for the lance corporal to return and that I was fine, and they would head off. But everybody that passed stopped; they were Marines and it was second nature to them to help out a comrade in trouble. I actually felt safer stranded where I was, on an unmarked desert road in the middle of nowhere, than I would have felt in the same circumstances on any highway in the United States. These guys would always be there to help me if I needed it. They would give their lives for you if it came down to it, but at the moment I was very content to sit and wait. I tried turning the hazards on and off to see if that had any effect on them pulling over, but it didn't, so I just left them off.

When the trucks were gone and I couldn't hear them or see their lights at all on the horizon, that is when it was the best. The desert was beautiful. The sky shone brightly in the north. Low clouds of smoke were lit with the flames of the burning oil fires in Kuwait.

About a half an hour later, I saw the lights of a single vehicle coming up from down south. The vehicle pulled over when it got to me. It was Gunney Hendrix's Blazer, and out stepped the big man himself, smiling as usual.

"Sir, what you got yourself into?"

For all the differences and arguments I had had with him in the past, I couldn't have been more happy to see him. He was like an old friend that night, and I felt a special bond with him out there on the empty plain that I'll never forget. Staff Sergeant James and Staff Sergeant Lynnwood were with him, and we all just waited there, shooting the bull, talking, laughing, and taking it easy. Hendrix gave me some Del Monte canned peaches in the little snack pack containers from the chow hall, and they waited with me until Pollock showed up about fifteen minutes later.

I told them to head out and check on Scott and Flynn, who had passed by earlier on their way into camp, and to tell them that I would see them in the morning. Pollock was already working on getting the bad tire off our vehicle while his buddy, a staff sergeant, was loosening the spare on the CUCV they had showed up in. I tried helping them do this and started banging away at the encrusted dirt and sand inside the wheel rim to get at the air valve, when bang, I knocked the valve stem off the air valve.

All the air started leaking out of the good tire, the one the staff sergeant and Lance Corporal Pollock were just getting ready to put on. Frantically I tried to plug it up and undo my stupidity, but it wasn't working. All I accomplished doing this was slicing up my thumb on the broken valve, and the air kept hissing out loud enough for the whole desert to hear. I apologized to the both of them, thinking this was a typical lieutenant-type thing to do.

("Don't let the lieutenant do it, he'll just fuck it up.")

Despite all my best efforts at screwing up their night, both Pollock and the staff sergeant just seemed to take this all in stride. "No big deal, sir, we can take care of it." To be honest, I don't know if I would have been as gracious in their stead, but I'll remember this the next time things go bad and I feel like lashing out at the nearest person I can lay the blame on.

Pollock did take care of it. While I was standing there like a fool with his thumb up his butt Pollock MacGyvered the thing. He used MRE gum to plug the broken valve, which stopped the hissing, and put the tire on the vehicle. He knew this wouldn't last, so we jumped in the truck quickly and headed back to try and get as far as we could before the leak started up again.

It worked for a while, at least until we had to jump the rough sand median that separated the dirt roads. Lance Corporal Pollock was pretty tired, and I guess he was having a hard time paying attention to the road and his driving. I didn't realize this, of course, until he kept going toward another vehicle that was coming straight for us.

"Whoa! Whoa! Whoa!"

Pollock woke up out of his daze and swerved right to avoid the oncoming lights. Up and over the median, and then the tire gave out.

It didn't take long before the tire went flat, but we kept going. We rode about twenty miles at 5 mph on the tire rim, totally destroying the tire by the time we got in. Pollock's boss was not a happy camper. But I answered as I was supposed to when he asked what happened and how the new tire went flat so quickly. "The second was a bad tire too?"

"Yup." Well, Pollock saved me from looking like an idiot on that one. Who says the troops don't take care of their lieutenants?

Today I woke up and decided to take Flynn and Scott out on the new route. They would be the best ones to tell me if it was any good, and if it was better than the old route. I tried to get Gunney Hendrix to do a recon on it to see if he thought it was a good idea and then have him send the other drivers down it if he did, but he was too busy getting blown-out tractor trailers back to Al Mishab.

So we headed off down the road, Scott and I in the one truck, Flynn and her A-driver in the other. Flynn had a big rig, with a blue cab. Scott and I were in a 5-ton. Scott is always cool to drive with. Young, eager, wears his heart on his sleeve. I can see him as an older Marine Corps vet, telling war stories about the Saudis. "In the big one."

At the turn where Pollock and I left all the big markers the night before saying to go south, I decided to go straight and see where that would take us. The road stretched off to the horizon and appeared to run east, roughly parallel with the Al Mishab road. If we were lucky, the road would continue that way, maybe head a little southeast, and come out right at Al Mishab. I even thought I knew where it came out, at the other turnoff outside the Al Mishab gate that ran west into the desert. This road might be one and the same. Whoever put it here, Army, Marines or Saudis, must have put it here to get somewhere, and where else could that be but Al Mishab?

I asked Flynn and Scott if they were comfortable with this. The road was semi-paved, and it might lead to Mishab. It could be a whole lot quicker than going the extra twenty miles south, so they went for it.

We cruised down the road after tightening the load on Flynn's truck, which was working itself loose on the bumpy roads, even though it was so heavy that it probably wouldn't go anywhere even without the straps. Finally after ten miles, we pulled around a bend and into a Saudi military outpost. The road just ended at the outpost.

I got out to talk with the Saudi soldiers to try and find out if this was the end of the road or if it went on further to Al Mishab. They must have been moving or something because there was stuff everywhere and they were carrying things out to their trucks from inside the building. The place looked like a little fort. Actually that is probably what it was. There were shrapnel marks and holes all over it, especially the garage. The Saudis saw us, and a few started over. One held out his hand. I took it and shook it warmly, trying to let him feel my goodwill through the handshake.

Talking was difficult at first, but another fellow came up who spoke passable English. I spoke to him and through him to everybody else. I asked them where the road went. They said it went on to Al Khafji. So I had been wrong, it wasn't running parallel to the Al Mishab-Al Khanjar road. It was leading us about twenty miles out of our way, north of Al Mishab. They offered us all tea, which I declined, and we took our leave. They were friendly and seemed happy enough to talk to us, but they were busy, and as we were leaving, they went right back to work.

So back to the intersection and south to the Al Mishab road, which was the way the Saudi soldier had told me we would have to go if we wanted to get to Al Mishab the quickest way.

We drove on until we hit the Al Mishab-Al Khanjar road just south of Al Kibrit, where we had some FARP sites set up. I'd seen their lights in the darkness last night with Lance Corporal Pollock, and we used them to get a fix on where we were. In the daytime you couldn't see the positions as clearly, because the landing lights didn't show up as they did at night. At night the place really did look like a beacon, even from the road. I guess that is what the pilots need when they are coming in for forward refuelling in the middle of the desert.

I had Flynn and Scott drop me off at the intersection, and I waited for the next vehicle to come by so I could hitch a ride back to Al Khanjar. It didn't take long. Hitchhiking out here is much easier than it is back home. There are no mass murderers or serial killers you need to worry about, and everybody you bump into is a Marine.

I hitched a ride with four guys in a HUMMV from Landing Support Battalion. The front and back seats were full, so I climbed in the very back, in what passes for the HUMMV's trunk. They had the plastic top up and buttoned, but dust still poured in the back from the road, and the ride was painful as hell, to say the least. I was slamming up and down on hard steel, and on one bump I thought I had broken my funny bone I came down on it so hard. I was afraid of hurting my back if that kept up, so I grabbed a rolled-up sleeping bag they had there and draped myself over it, bracing my legs against the back of the HUMMV's rear gate. This way I could absorb all the bouncing around better and wouldn't hurt myself slamming up and down on the steel floor of the HUMMV.

And these were the same roads I rode up last night with Pollock? That I thought were pretty good? It sure makes a difference where and what you travel in when you are forming an opinion on road conditions. Don't ask me what I think of those roads now.

I got back just in time to run into Major Brown, who had come up to check on the move and find out why it was taking so long. (Seems they want the matting moved faster than it's possible to do with the assets we have, and they are going to keep pushing even if it isn't doing any good.) I filled Major Brown in on the run, probably making it sound worse than was actually the case, because I wasn't exactly sure how it was going myself.

Major Brown wanted to know how the convoys were running. Who made up the schedule for the runs and what trucks went in what convoys? Were the drivers getting the proper food, water, and rest? And everything else that is usually involved with convoy operations. I couldn't answer most of the questions he asked because I didn't know how it was running, which was my own fault, so he said he would wait until Gunney Hendrix got in and then clear things up with him.

Gunney Hendrix took a while getting back, and Major Brown wanted the operation organized better and brought under control, so he began holding on to the trucks and staging them as they came in. This way he could get a look at them, find out how many convoys there were, and send them off in regular groups instead of just individually. He also wanted to make sure 273 did a better job of supporting the drivers. Word had gotten back that they weren't sleeping enough or getting enough rest, that they weren't able to shower, and that they were eating MREs almost three times a day. Most of this was untrue, but everything seemed so disorganized there was no way to prove it.

Coleman told me later what had happened. Apparently 271 had complained that we weren't taking care of their drivers. They were the ones whose truck was missing the night we came up here, and they said we left them out there for over twenty hours, which was an outright lie. They also claimed their drivers were getting no food, no rest, and no break for days on end. The truth of the matter is that 271 didn't want to be involved in the move and used all these complaints as justification to pull their trucks.

The first thing Staff Sergeant James had done when he got up to Al Khanjar was to let Captain Daley know about the broken-down truck. A wrecker was sent out, and every vehicle going down that way we had come up was told to look for it. There is also no way a truck could be broken down on that road for that long without somebody stopping to help. It just wouldn't happen. What the drivers did was to pull off the road behind a sand dune, wait until the convoy was well past, and then head back to 271 at Tanajib. And this was the same truck that was trying to get out of going in the first place. Now they were trying to screw us by saying we had just left them there.

As for the other stuff, well, there were a few problems there, but nothing like 271 made them out to be. Captain Daley and his people were busting their ass trying to support the drivers. They always had hot chow ready when the drivers came in at night or in the morning, and they went out of their way to help them out whenever they could. The one problem they did have was with the sleeping arrangements. If any of the drivers wanted to sleep in one of the two available tents, which weren't enough to house all the drivers in the first place, they had to sleep on a bare, rocky floor because there weren't any cots for them. Most of them preferred to sleep in their cabs anyway, but for those who didn't, there weren't any cots, and this was definitely an oversight on our part.

The convoys who knew the situation brought their own cots up, and this is where we could have done things better. All the convoys and convoy commanders should have been briefed prior to coming up here on what they would be hauling and what they would need to haul and support themselves in the process. But as usual we just told the units we needed trucks up at Al Khanjar ASAP, and the drivers were sent up with no brief, no idea what was going on, and generally nothing of what they needed to make themselves comfortable. They didn't even know to whom to report half the time.

Gunney Hendrix had decided to send the trucks off individually or in whatever units they wanted to go because it made things a whole lot easier to control. Drivers could go at their own pace, which is a hell of a lot easier than driving in a convoy. They avoided building up the dust clouds that always resulted from traveling together and proved to be so dangerous. There was no long waiting period at either end while the trucks were loaded and unloaded, which would have been the case if they had come in in convoys. They could stop at the PX on the way and grab something to eat there, which Flynn did all the time because she wanted to, not because she had to. And they could grab showers at the halfway point.

The only thing this didn't do was ensure that all the drivers were doing the work they were supposed to. You could screw off if you felt like it, and nobody could really catch you. So it meant trusting the drivers much more. But I believe if the drivers knew what they were moving and why, and that when they finished they would be that much closer to going home, then there would be no problems with them goofing off.

The two things that Gunney Hendrix did get wrong were having no idea of what trucks or convoys were running and his penchant for changing things around and playing the tyrant with the drivers. Almost all the drivers were pissed off at him for one reason or another, and he did make decisions that often made no sense or just plain put people out, like switching Scott from one truck to another when he pulled in for the morning and sending him right back out.

But Gunney Hendrix was doing his best as he saw fit, and the move was going along as well as could be expected with what we had to work with. Explaining all this to Major Brown made me realize what Gunney Hendrix was actually trying to do. So once the major left with Coleman, after seeing Hendrix and leaving instructions with him to gather up all the trucks, let them stay the night, and get them launched in an organized fashion in the morning, I decided to let things run the way they had been running and get the trucks loaded up and on their way ASAP.

That way we wouldn't lose the twelve hours we would if we held the trucks here over night. Many of the drivers were ready to go and pissed off that they were just sitting there, so they were more than happy to load up and get one more run in before it got too late to do so. The drivers would usually sleep where they were in the early morning hours and keep driving at all other times.

I guess it's a sort of rhythm they got into, though Scott was telling me that once Gunney Hendrix had him on the road so long he couldn't see straight, let alone drive. I have to be careful with these guys.

We decided the only thing we would do differently would be to keep a list of all the trucks and convoys that went out, the time they left, the names of the drivers and A-drivers, and the names of the convoy commanders if they went in a convoy. The drivers were the ones who decided how they wanted to go. If they had come up as part of a convoy and had somebody in charge who knew what he was doing, they went as a convoy. That was easy. If they didn't come up as part of a convoy, they could either join one or go on their own. The real hard chargers, who hated working with anybody and preferred to just drive on their own, loaded up and set out whenever they saw fit.

So basically I let the drivers run themselves, which I hoped would get them fired up and make them work that much harder.

Gunney and I were now together on this. I saw what he was up to, and he figured out where I could help him. He kept on the road scrounging parts and troubleshooting, looking for broken-down vehicles and calling to check on them if they were hours late so Captain Daley's wrecker could go and fix them up. Meanwhile I logged the convoys in and out, tried to make the drivers' lives a little more comfortable, and generally kept track of what was going on.

16 March 1991

I woke up the next day feeling a whole lot better about things. Now at least I had a handle on what was going on and knew how to get things moving. This is what I should have known coming up here, not three days later. It's hard to know what to do in a situation like this. Should I have stepped in earlier? Tried to be more of a player on the 273 side? Gotten Gunney Hendrix under control the minute I got up here? When I asked Staff Sergeant James, he told me to let Gunney Hendrix keep on running things, that he was doing okay. Flynn and Scott told me he was all screwed up, and the captain and the major said he was a royal pain in the ass. Then Major Brown came up and said 273 was all screwed up. So what the hell is the solution? At least now we have a plan.

So I'm finally getting a feel for what I'm doing and I'm waiting for the convoys that went out late last night to return, when over the radio I hear Jerry Healey calling me. Our replacements have arrived. Right when we figure out what we're doing we are on our way home. Everybody. Me, Gunney Hendrix, Staff Sergeant James, and Staff Sergeant Lynnwood. All of us bummed, thinking that we might have done something wrong, wishing that we could stay for only a few more days and finish what we had started. There really wasn't that much left to go of the matting. Over 70% of it had been moved, and in two more days the rest of it would be out of here, only we wouldn't be here to see it.

Did Colonel Caldwell think we had screwed up? Did he need me back to work on the radios? Were we going back to give him a progress report? To defend ourselves against 271's accusations? I spent the rest of the day filling in Jerry, Peter, John, and Top Riley, all of whom had come up to run this thing, and waiting for Gunney Hendrix to show up so we could go home. I had no vehicle to get home with myself and had been getting around walking and bumming rides.

We had started out the move with eighteen tractor trailers and about twenty-eight 5-tons, and were down to twelve tractor trailers and eighteen 5-tons, and vehicles were still going down all the time. Gunney Hendrix was doing all he could to keep them up, however.

What Jerry and the others did was to stage all the vehicles as they came in and tell the drivers and convoy commanders to relax for a while. They were going to run three convoys. There would be twelve tractor trailers in one with Peter Hart as convoy commander, twelve 5-tons in another with John Clark as convoy commander, and the six MWSS-174 trucks in the last with the regular convoy commander in charge. Top Riley got control of all the vehicles and drivers and was out late doing it, but that is the kind of thing he loves doing and does very well. It helps to have a good staff NCO helping you out. Jerry didn't have to worry about keeping track of the trucks at all, which was one of my biggest pains in the ass. Top Riley kept good accountability of all the convoy information and left Jerry free to run things.

MWSS-174 also arrived ready to conduct twenty-four hour ops. They had left a few days ago to go to a party they were having down at King Abdul Aziz, by order of their squadron commander, and were back now ready to do business. They had two complete crews of drivers and A-drivers who would switch off duties while the other half rested. They had cots and everything else they needed to stay up here for a while and were ready to go. That is the way you do things.

They all thought Staff Sergeant Lynnwood was supposed to be at Al Mishab accounting for the matting coming in and were surprised when he wasn't. Was he supposed to be there or not? I don't know. That was Brady's call.

Jerry jumped right on getting more tents, except he still doesn't have cots to go with them. That will be my job when I get back to King Abdul Aziz. Finally Gunney Hendrix arrived, and we made plans to leave the next morning.

17 March 1991

At dawn we got up, made sure everything was going okay, got last minute messages from Jerry and the others for Colonel Caldwell, and took off. We stopped at Maintenance Battalion to get our vehicle fixed for some little problem and then finally got on the road for home.

About a mile out, we passed the first convoy heading south. I counted 8 tractor trailers as we went by; this out of the 12 that were supposed to be there. I guess Jerry and the others were already getting a taste of what we had had to deal with up here.

Captain Daley had pulled me aside just before we left. I think he saw I was kind of in the dumps about getting sent home with the job half done, and he told me that me and my crew had done fine. He said that there were lots of ways to run convoys, and one wasn't any better than another. It's what you want to accomplish with the one you choose that is important, and if they had wanted more control over the movement, they should have made that clear in the first place.

By staging the trucks all night, sending them out together at 0800, and expecting them to arrive at Al Mishab for offload in their convoy formations, they were using up a lot of time. Which is fine if that is what they wanted to do, but that should have been the plan from the beginning. It definitely didn't make things go any faster, so I don't know why they went to that plan anyway if the time crunch was the big problem. Especially if they are only doing one run a day.

On the way back we all sort of sat there and bummed. We kept thinking we had screwed up somehow and hadn't gotten the job done as we were supposed to. (Later Colonel Caldwell told us: "You boys did fine. If you had had the support you needed, you would have been done by Saturday." But at the time we had no idea what he thought, and we were afraid we had let him down.) Then I started working on our brief. I got Gunney Hendrix, Staff Sergeant James, and Staff Sergeant Lynnwood involved, and we started putting together a briefing outline that would let Colonel Caldwell know what we had done up there.

So much of the military, or of life, is being able to explain what is going on, or what has happened and why. If you can explain things to somebody, give them an idea or a model of the problem, then you are more than halfway home on making things happen and making a name for yourself. I realized then, sitting in the Blazer going home, that this was just like writing. You can actually make up a specific reality or truth by the elements you choose to describe it. A painter's brush strokes define the image projected and direct the viewer's impression of it. So too with writing. Whatever you put down, the things you include as well as what you leave out, these all paint the picture you want the reader to form of your subject.

All we had to do was show Colonel Caldwell that we had a plan and how it worked. There was a plan that was in effect up there, but if you asked Gunney Hendrix, who had developed it, what it was, he couldn't have told you. He was just sort of running things on instinct, which is how most things happen. Now it was my job to codify that plan and make it verbal. To give words to the ideas that he had but couldn't express.

This is where we failed before. With Major Brown I didn't know what was going on, and Gunney Hendrix had nothing to show him to explain it, so it looked like chaos. Now we had lists of trucks and drivers, a method to what was going on, and specific problems we had run into trying to accomplish the mission. We were shaping what had happened into something that made sense, that had order, reason, purpose. By the time we finished, it looked as if we were conducting a viable and fully capable motor transport operation.

We even made it look as if the way we were running the convoys actually worked, which now I'm even starting to believe.

On the way out of the camp, we saw a dog wrestling with a big, fat rat. The dog would keep grabbing him with his teeth, trying to bite or crunch him, then let him go as the rat tried to bite back. Then the rat would scurry away a few feet, and the dog would try again. There were a bunch of Marines standing around watching this battle and cheering on the dog. I don't know if the rat got away or the dog finally killed him.

We stopped once on the Al Tareeg road to look at the sky up north, which was overcast and grey with oily black clouds from the fires in Kuwait, and got a few pictures of ourselves against the side of the truck with the sky heavy in the distance. The next stop we made was at Al Mishab, to check on Neulight, whose truck was broke down there, and the matting. Then home.

I rehearsed the debrief on the way back for the others, and they added whatever they thought we needed. The plan was that I would speak first, then they would elaborate if the colonel wanted details, which I was sure he would. So when we got back and went into Colonel Caldwell's office, we were ready. The road dust, the three-day growth, and our overall dirty appearance probably helped. The brief went as follows:

• We began on Tuesday with 1,993 bundles of AM-2 matting to get to Al Mishab.

• By Saturday at 1700 we had 703 bundles left to go. (This didn't include the ones already loaded on trucks and staged, but still at Al Khanjar. We counted those in the bundles that had been moved to Al Mishab.)

• We started out with eighteen tractor trailers. By Saturday at 1700, eleven of these were still up and the other seven were down. One was down on the lot, one was down at the port, one was down at Al Mishab, one was jackknifed in the desert, one was down at 271, and two were down on the road.

• Of the units involved, MWSS-273 had six 5-tons with one down. MWSS-374 had six 5-tons and one LVS with three down. And MWSS-174 had four 5-tons ready for 24 hour ops 14–16 March. They had been up earlier but had gone back for a squadron party on Wednesday. They came back on Friday with their two crews ready to begin the 24-hour op schedule.

• Wrecker (Hub Cap) was sent back to 374 with a downed vehicle. The people we sent back were supposed to get cots and send them back to Lonesome Dove so the drivers would have something to sleep on.

• Gunney Hendrix ran some small convoys consisting of two or more trucks and also let some trucks go individually. The trucks showed up, loaded up, went to Al Mishab and were unloaded there by forklift operators who were standing by as the trucks pulled in. The drivers decided their own pace and how many runs they would get in per day.

• Gunney Hendrix was also responsible for keeping the trucks up. He cruised the roads between Lonesome Dove and Al Mishab looking for breakdowns and parts, troubleshooting, and helping out the drivers who got in any kind of trouble.

• Wreckers were dispatched from 273 as needed. Word would go to Captain Daley via Gunney Hendrix, the convoy commanders, or anybody else who knew our vehicles needed help.

We explained to the colonel that we had the following problems with the operation:

• MWSS-273 had no maintenance detachment at Lonesome Dove and no way of getting any repairs done on the trucks.

• Chow was not a problem, despite what the 271 CO said. The drivers got breakfast and dinner, and dinner was available anytime from 1700 on.

• We had two tents for the drivers, but no cots. That is what we sent Hub Cap back for.

• The only showers they had there were drip showers.

• Truckers took showers at Al Mishab or at other stops along the way.

In short, we told the colonel that we counted on the individual truckers to exercise their own initiative and responsibility, and we allowed them to run things as they wanted to. The procedures our replacements were setting up when we left cut down the individual driver's role in the operation and established greater command and control measures over the move itself. Warrant Officer Hart was running one convoy of eleven tractor trailers, while Warrant Officer Clark was running another of twelve 5-tons. MWSS-174 had their own convoy with six 5-tons. They planned to dispatch a wrecker with each convoy. (Since there were only two, this probably didn't come off; Captain Daley needed one at Lonesome Dove the whole time if any of the trucks he was running went down.) They hoped to get in one run a day for each convoy.

Jerry also got extra tents from the 273 people as they moved out. He estimated completing the move in three days, with one day for cleanup. After we told Colonel Caldwell various items our replacements needed, Gunney Hendrix, Staff Sergeant James, Staff Sergeant Lynnwood, and I fielded the rest of the questions he had.

When the briefing was all done, Colonel Caldwell said we had done a fine job and told us to go get cleaned up. Staff Sergeant James said we had got our point across. Gunney Hendrix did his big, chipping in at opportune moments, and the whole thing seemed to have come off pretty well.

The truth of the whole matter was that the move was a little out of control, but it was proceeding and getting done. It wasn't as organized as I had made it out to be, but neither was it as disorganized as Major Brown went away thinking that night he came up to check on things. In both cases, however, the way we presented it was the way they presumed it was going. Our grasp of it all and ability to explain it was the key element in their perception of how well we were handling it.

I guess that is why Schwarzkopf is where he is and why everybody is so impressed with how the war went. When he talks, it's like getting beaten over the head with what is going on. You have no doubts but that he is firmly in control of everything that is happening and that there is a master plan somewhere that is working like clockwork.

Lessons learned:

1. Always get accountability immediately of whatever it is you are working with. Men, machines, equipment, etc. Accountability gives you control and direction. If you have a list in front of you, it makes it a whole lot easier to figure out what needs to be done next.

2. Make sure the Marines are taken care of, which is easier said than done when you have nothing to take care of them with. But be creative and scrounge around for ideas or materials to make this happen.

3. Don't wait for things to happen. You have to make them happen. Again this is easy to write down but hard to do. (I should have set up a movement control center right off, but I let things just roll along.) Have an idea of what needs to be done and do it. At the same time don't go trampling all over a system that is already working or take initiative away from people around you who are trying their best to get things set up and running at the same time you are.

4. Knowledge is knowing what needs to be done and considerations to be taken into account in different situations. Much of this can come from common sense, but experience is always invaluable.

5. Don't be afraid of the "system." Usually the system is just a way to get people to think about things and help them get going when something needs to be done. Don't ever let it become a limiting factor.

6. Adapt the plan to the situation. You can't always do what you want. Do what you can.

7. Be patient. Many of the troubles we had came down to wanting the matting moved faster than it could be in the circumstances. If there is a real need to get something done fast, then so be it. If not, let it happen in an appropriate amount of time.

8. The key to much of this is being able to balance your role as an officer with your role in a specific operation, or at least walking a fine line between the two. That is where the real trouble is and the thing that is hardest to do when you are given a job to get done.

18 March 1991

The lights came on in the stadium tonight. The whole place is lit up like a parking lot at a football game. Walking over the grounds behind the tents, where all traces of the bunkers have been wiped out, I couldn't help but think about how strange and emotionally confusing this whole war has been.

There was so much tension and initial shock at the fact that we would actually be in a war. Then it came with lightning speed, though at the time it seemed as if the days were just dragging along with endless speculation about how things were going. Our work seemed so far removed from the actual war effort that it was hard to relate to the larger picture.

Then it was over, and we experienced the easing of that tension, the catharsis of emotion that it had all ended so easily and successfully, at such a small cost to our forces. The whole thing seemed like a dream. I'm sure this is what people at home are thinking too, what Maryanne feels, and Mom, Dad, Kerry, and even Ryan. He doesn't realize in his disappointment about not being over here that it wasn't really about blood, guts, and glory, but little jobs and constant bewilderment at Saddam's "weird war."

Now the time is flying by. The war seems far, far away. Concerns of home and plans for the future have again become the dominant poles in our lives, and speculation about the war and what might have been is fading fast. With the lights on, especially, it seems that it is really over. The tension that was running beneath the surface is gone, completely vanished, and we are even forgetting how serious this all was when it first started. It's a done deal now, and it will go down differently than any of us ever imagined. All anybody wants to do now is get home.

The lights reminded me of all this. Seeing the night lit up for the first time in who knows how long made me remember going out dancing, going to the movies, playing baseball under the lights, and everything else that you normally do at home in the evening without ever thinking about it.

You can go to the showers now and see where you are going, even on the way back. You can walk through the tents in the parking lot and not get your head taken off by a tent line or stretch of comm wire you didn't see. And best of all, you can hear the troops playing pick-up basketball again at night while you are lying in the rack or falling off to sleep. You can hear them dribbling, the ball hitting the rim or bouncing off the backboard, their talk, laughter, and their endless taunting of one another. They are living again and not thinking of war or scud missile attacks.

The lights remind me of life, of home, and of our parents' joy and relief that soon their beloved sons and daughters will be coming home heroes. This is such a long way from Vietnam, which is what we have been taught to measure things by since I've been in the Marine Corps, and so like a strange, bewildering dream I still don't know what to make of it all.

19 March 1991

Today was an adventurous day, to say the least. And once again I've been saved from a bad situation by Allah, or God, or whoever is up there looking out for me.

Colonel Staunton asked me to take down MAG-13's repeater, which is positioned on the top of the stadium roof. I grabbed Kevin, who was good enough to help out, and we headed over to the stadium after the Tyson fight was over. Then we got in touch with Jim Flobeck, the communications officer, his compadre, Walt, Staff Sergeant Reyna, the communications chief, and Lance Corporal Neulight, who is now back at 174. They were going to show us the way up there and help us get the thing down. Staff Sergeant Reyna was the big Kahuna in this deal; he had put the thing up there and knew what the hell he was doing. I had no idea. He told me it was a bitch, though, getting it up there, and it would be just as hard getting it down.

The actual repeater was no problem. That was on the top floor of the stadium, and all we had to do was lug it out and down to the truck. The antennas were going to be the pain. They were on the roof itself, and we had to go up through a skylight to get them and lower them down through it.

They took us up to the fourth deck, then rigged up their contraption to get us to the roof. They put one table on top of another table, then a wooden ladder on top of that, which led through the skylight and to the roof. While Staff Sergeant Reyna, Neulight, and I made the 30-foot climb up to the roof, the other guys started taking out the repeater.

We all got up all right, got down the antennas, and passed them back down through the skylight to Kevin and the others waiting below. Kevin came up while we were working on the last one. We got that down, did a little looking around, and noticed the roof was cracked in a few places and slippery with dirt and sand. It wasn't the safest place in the world. I thought it even looked as if it might collapse at some point in the not too distant future, so I decided it was time to head back down.

I had a bad feeling about the ladder, so I thought I would go first in case anything happened. I took the two metal clamps that were used to connect the antennas to the antenna pole, let Staff Sergeant Reyna and Neulight grab the antenna pole, and started down.

I still had this weird premonition about falling, and as I went down the first three steps I stopped for a minute to reposition my hands alongside the ladder so if it slipped they wouldn't get jammed in between the ladder and the edge of the skylight. Kevin was holding the ladder steady right above me, and everything seemed cool. All of a sudden I was falling. I thought to myself, "Relax — take it easy — you're falling." Then the ladder slammed onto the table, and I saw my left leg, which was caught between the slats, hit hard against the bottom of the slat above it as I fell backwards. The whole thing bounced off the table, me, the ladder, and everything else, and I jumped up and out before I came back down.

I was terrified that I had broken my leg. Broken bones scare the hell out of me. Thinking of how fragile the body is and how easy it is to mangle it or smash it up always bums me out. Now I was too afraid to look under my pants leg for fear of what I would see. I kept walking around trying to feel if I was okay and to see if the pain in my leg was only from it hitting so hard on the ladder rung. I was definitely whacked out. I kept saying, "I'm okay! I'm okay! Thank God!" The adrenalin must have been raging because a few minutes later I was feeling lightheaded and nauseous.

I lay down while some of Flobeck's comm guys ran for a corpsman, who was luckily only stationed a little ways away in the medical station downstairs. I was still terrified I had broken my leg and was afraid to look at it, but after a while I got up the courage and pulled up my pant leg. Thank God, and praise be to Allah. It looked okay. Badly bruised, but probably not broken, unless it was a hairline fracture or something.

Another Marine looked at it, and then the corpsman, who twisted it left and right, then back and forth to make sure it wasn't broken. After that I felt better, and they helped me down to medical, where the doctor took a look at it. When he said it wasn't broken, I felt much better. Finally I stopped worrying and thanked God for not making it worse. Just thinking about the trauma that the leg did go through, all the tissue damage and the pressure that must have been on it, was making me sick, but once the doctor told me the leg was good to go, I was up again and walking out to find Kevin and see what was up with the repeater.

After an accident the best thing you can do if the damage isn't really major or deeply traumatic is to get back on your feet again and use or exercise the injured area. I learned this rowing. Whenever you babied something, it took longer to heal. Getting blood flowing through it and oxygenating it definitely speeds up the healing process.

Kevin was very relieved when he saw me. So was Jim, Walt, Staff Sergeant Reyna, Neulight, and all the rest. Since everything turned out okay, we could now joke about it, about what an oaf I was and how I must have been too fat to use the ladder. "We've been up there a bunch a times and nothing happens. You go up once and wham! the whole thing comes down. What have you been eating, Sean? You better start PTing again fast."

Kevin was laughing about seeing me fall spread eagled in front of him, and then at me jumping up so fast, saying, "I'm okay, everything's fine." Almost forcing everything to be that way.

Now I know why they are always talking about safety. Here I am, an officer, supposed to be looking out for my men and not letting them go up bullshit like that, and I go ahead and do just that.

Man! Lucky again. God must be looking out for me.

Hoss got hurt earlier today, too. A 5-ton ran into his 5-ton when he pulled the convoy he was leading off the road to wait for stragglers. I guess the dust was so bad that the driver of the rear truck didn't know the others had stopped and kept right on going through them. He hit Hoss's truck at an angle, knocking Hoss back into the cab and ripping the entire flat bed off his own 5-ton. If John had fallen the other way when the truck hit he would be dead right now. Man, all these accidents. And the stinkin' war is over. Seems as if it's more dangerous now than it was when the war was going on.

This is probably to be expected because people are that much more careless now and not thinking about what they are doing. We are too antsy to get home and not keeping our minds on the fact that things can still get pretty hairy around here.

After the whole thing with the accident, I went back to the Group HQ to settle down a bit and rest. I had Kevin help me put the repeater in the conex box we use to hold all the radio equipment, and that is where it will sit for the time being, all safe and sound until I get the chance to pack it up and embark it out of here, which I have to figure out how to do. But now Stocks has something else for me to do, and as usual it is totally out of my area of expertise and I don't know how the hell I'm going to get it done.

He wants me to draft up a plan of the King Abdul Aziz airfield. It is actually a surveying and drafting project, but Tony told him I could draw because he has seen me practicing with the drawing kit Maryanne gave me, and now I'm supposed to get it done. Like I can actually draw the airfield and make it look as they want it to.

But no worries. The squadrons have a surveying and drafting section, and I just went over to 174 and scrounged up plans they already had made up. What they had was actually somebody's personal project on the airfield. All the other stuff they had made up has long since vanished, and this guy kept the one as a memento. So I borrowed that, and then had Sergeant McEntire take me over to one of the Seabee camps to get them reproduced.

We found what we needed at Camp 13; they had the big machines you use to reproduce blueprints, and we asked them if they could reproduce the plans we had. The Seabees are great. Any of them will bust their ass for you and do whatever you need done. Of course they did it, and they even kept fooling with the thing to get it to come out the best it could. I grabbed them some cokes from the PX across the way in return for helping us out, and we headed home with another mission completed.

Cards tonight. Warrant Officer Peter Hart, "Lizard," was smoking everyone as usual. There is no beating him. He is always first on the table with his card, the first done sorting out his hand, and the first to know what the hell he is doing. He is the only person I've ever met who can pick whom he is going to drop his hearts on and get away with it, or drop any of his cards on for that matter, even spades when we are playing that. We all just sit there playing, swapping jokes about the war and English's adventures, while Peter kicks our ass. And he is the one usually telling the stories.

Major Brown leaves tonight. I hope the rest of us will be out of here around mid-April, although May 9 is the planned date now.

As I wait to go home, I wonder about many things. Why does the rear get gear before the front line units do, if they even get it at all? We all have our desert boots and desert cammies, and many of the grunts still don't have theirs. Some of the frontline units did their assault in their jungle cammies because they didn't have any of the desert ones to wear. I also know that many of the grunts aren't even getting boots; now that the war is over they are not issuing them out anymore, and those that didn't get them are out of luck.

One Marine got caught trying to mail home three pair, and he was wearing one pair. They asked him how he got so many pairs of boots. "I have connections in Supply," he answered. They confiscated the boots, as they should have, but I wonder how many more people have already gotten their stuff past the system. How many other desert boots have been ripped off and mailed home to augment some Marine's personal stash?

John said he saw a box of size 5½ desert boots, and a bunch of other boxes full of desert cammies spilled all over the road up at Al Khanjar when he was up there a few days ago. I wonder how many Marines who could have used that stuff are going without it right now?

Stewart MacDonald, MWSS-174 motor transport officer, believes the Marine Corps is critically short of motor transport assets and is entirely dependent on civilian assets to make up for the shortfalls. Besides this, the stuff we do have is too small. Our trucks and LVSs should be 40' size, tractor-trailer size, instead of being only one container length long.

He also said it was stupid to have ordered all Marine corps personnel to use Jet A-1 as the only fuel source, "to prove that we are an amphibious force with amphibious capabilties." MacDonald said the stuff destroys motors, generators, and everything else they used it in, despite what HQMC states. He says that the Marines were always sneaking in diesel or Mogas to keep their vehicles up.

Lonesome Dove airfield was built from scratch. The biggest airfield ever built totally from the ground up in a combat environment. But even with our ability to construct such a thing, Gunner Gilroy, the MWSS-273 EAF officer, says it's always much more practical and efficient to build on or add to an airfield which already exists, as at King Abdul Aziz, Shaikh Isa, etc.

There are rumors that planes are leaving for home empty. Open seats are being announced all the time over the radios, but nobody is ready to go and the seats are staying empty. Only a few nights ago MAG-13 was told at the last minute there was a bunch of seats available on a flight home, but Marines wanting to leave had to be at the airport in three hours. So MAG-13 jumped through the hoops getting people packed up and out to the airport only to find when they got out there that a mistake had been made in the scheduling and the seats were not all available. It turned out only half the seats they were told they had were actually theirs to take. So half of MAG-13 got out while the other half went back to King Abdul Aziz to wait for the next leap-ex.

Some psycho Marine up north tried to ship home a human arm. Now the customs people are going through everything that is getting sent home and picking out whatever contraband they find. So far they have been finding grenades, live rounds, mines, Iraqi war gear and weapons, and anything else you can think of that the Marines are getting their hands on up there. I guess the lucky ones have already sent their stuff home.

Moving out. A whole new set of requirements. Tires for vehicles, cleaning, staging, etc. Knowing what needs to be done, the questions to ask, what to be concerned with — this is what gives you direction, and what is going to get us out of here a whole lot faster.

22 March 1991

My birthday is coming up!

Got word the other day that General Schwarzkopf might need the 2d Marine Division to stay and that they would need an ACE to support them, which might mean 30 days to 6 months until we're out of here.

I've been reading *Newsweek* and getting a sense of just how big this war was and everything that went into it, such as the Army armored units that engaged Republican Guard units after the cease-fire. Don't ever think this victory wasn't paid for.

I'm getting impatient with the Motorolas. They are coming in and going out now almost faster than I can keep accounting for them, and Colonel Staunton just told me to get two more mobiles set up. Problem is that nobody knows how to do it. Hewitt is back at 174, and our new comm guys don't want anything to do with the Motorolas.

Read Hall's *Life* and *U.S. News and World Report* earlier. Lots of pictures of service men and women returning home. The ones with the fathers being welcomed back by their wives and children cut especially close. All the people there to meet them, all the ribbons and support, man that makes you feel good. I hope that will be us stepping off the planes in a few more weeks.

Yesterday two majors showed up from Headquarters Marine Corps in Washington, D.C., as part of a battle damage assessment team. They came by to get a look at all our records and to take back as much as possible to study later.

This is what I briefed the major and his partner on when asked for personal observations:

I. First I explained our mission and how the MWSG was set up. I told them that we fulfilled all the 3D MAW ground support requirements through our subordinate units, the Marine wing support squadrons, which were assigned to a MAG at every major air station, and that we did this directly for the 3d MAW commander and his staff and subordinate elements.

II. Observations.

A. Trucking — not enough USMC assets. Our priority with FSSG was very low, even though we had an important job to do, like everybody else, because the FSSG's priority was Division. The Marine Corps needs more trucks across the board, and bigger trucks. We can't possibly move everything we need to as fast as we need to do it with what we have now. If we hadn't had the Saudis to support us, we would have been dead in the water.

B. MPS — great system, but needs more control over offload evolution and distribution of gear. If that had been the case, MPS would have been perfect. Also, Division can't be allowed to hoard all the assets.

C. Why use Jet A-1 in the vehicle systems? It destroys vehicles, generators, and whatever else it is put into. Maybe the stuff we had to use was bad, or maybe the stuff is bad across the board. I've heard many different theories on this one.

D. FSSG overtaxed — too many requirements, not enough people. MWSG-37 became a mini-FSSG on numerous occasions out of necessity. Major Howard got item manager codes, did follow-up requests over the telephone (which effectively put the part on order), then used project codes to get the parts on the desert express. One part came in 72 hours after it was ordered. DPRs were 1½ to 2 weeks behind, so all the units adjusted themselves accordingly and pretty much did whatever they had to do to get what they needed. People at home busted their ass to support us. The log jam was in the FSSG requisition and filing system. Thousands of dollars of the FSSG's money was spent without its officers even knowing about it by aggressive units going after their parts requirements. Their motto: "Make the system work for you."

E. We did not always prevent problems in the field by using the systems developed in the rear, such as convoy operation systems and the full MIMMS cycle. People just did whatever because we were at war, and they could get away with it. Stuff didn't have time to come back on us. If it had we would have realized much of the stuff we were doing was flat-out wrong — wasteful and inefficient in the long run.

F. Comm was the pits. Who is responsible for buying this shit or determining the Marine Corps's comm requirements anyway? They do a real shitty job of it. Our comm systems are so antiquated it is ridiculous. At Al Jabar, Colonel Coop couldn't talk down the road. An Air Force sergeant pulled up, pulled out a briefcase, plugged it into his HUMMV battery, and talked to Riyadh. Half the time I couldn't talk to MWSS-174, which was only fifty yards away, but I never had a problem calling home.

G. Questions on ammo, water, fuel and supply support I really couldn't answer or comment on because I haven't had sufficient experience with those sections over here.

24 March 1991

Today was a slow, depressing day. Read, played some volleyball, and signed out some radios. Dinner with Kevin and John, swatting flies away. Kevin could tell I was in the dumps because I wasn't talking much. Usually I'm talking my head off.

I'm just depressed about feeling as if I'm going nowhere over here. I don't feel productive or as if I'm accomplishing anything. There is just nothing to do. No bars, no city or town to go to, no distractions, nothing. You just get up, eat, go to work, eat, work, eat, mess around in the tent at night, then sleep.

Saw *Die Hard 2* tonight. Cheered me up, even as awful as it was.

25 March 1991

Another day begins as usual with breakfast. Long line, then the walk to work. I think Corporal Flynn is pregnant because this morning she has been going through all sorts of emotional turmoil. Either crying or yelling, and snapping out at everybody, including Sergeant McEntire.

We'll see what the rest of the day holds.

MAG-26 CO to Colonel Coop, "Those radios were a lifesaver."

25 March 1991

At 2100, English came in and asked me if I wanted to go to a Ramadan feast with some Saudi Marine officers he had met. I said sure, and he told me to be ready to go by 2215. At 2200 I got dressed in a clean uniform and put on my new, unused desert boots, just as Corporal Saks came in to get me.

Saks, Corporal Aristide, Captain O'Brien, who as usual took forever to get ready, and I waited in the road by the second sentry post until a Saudi captain showed up to bring us to the tent where they were waiting for us at the Saudi naval base just down the road.

We cruised over, got a warm welcome from the Saudi soldiers, and sat down around the carpet to drink coffee and tea and eat dates. The senior captain had put on his Arab robes for us and patiently answered all of our questions on the coffee and tea drinking. Saks kept wanting to trade gear, and English was talking to the captain about the course of the war, while all the rest of the Saudi soldiers kept gathering around Aristide and getting their pictures taken with her.

Aristide seemed to be the hit of the whole thing. Through the captain, who was about the only person who could really speak English, the Saudi soldiers kept telling us they really wanted an American wife, which I'm sure was for Aristide's benefit as much as anything else.

The Saudi soldiers ranged in age from about twenty-one to thirty, but they all looked much younger, almost like kids. They all laughed and kissed each other as they arrived at the tent to celebrate Ramadan, and with them all there it made the whole gathering a lot of fun. There never was a feast, but the tea was awesome, and I drank more than my fill of it. There was a lieutenant there too who spoke pretty good English, and I spent most of my time talking to him and the captain about Saudi Arabia and Islam. They were delighted at how much I knew of their culture and asked me where I learned it all. "I read about it," I replied. They were very interested in what I had read and especially in what we Americans thought about their country.

At about 0115, we got up to go. We took a few more pictures, this time with the traditional Arab headresses on, traded some gear, and headed back. Aristide got into the cab of the truck we were heading back in, alongside the Saudi driver, and another of the Saudi soldiers, who looked about all of seventeen, jumped in beside her. Saks and I hopped in the back of the truck while English jumped in the captain's vehicle.

Aristide got the undivided attention of the two Saudi soldiers on the way back while I was doing my best just to give them directions. "Good. Good. Straight? Straight, yes, straight." They probably didn't understand a word I was saying, but they did manage to get us to where we were going, however they figured out the way to get there. I had Saks keep an eye on Aristide to make sure she was doing okay, and we cruised down the wet, gleaming street toward our camp.

They let us off at the first checkpoint, turned around, waved goodbye, and were gone. I asked Aristide what they had been talking to her about so exuberantly in the cab. She laughed and told me they'd wanted to come back and see her again tomorrow. And with that we went off to our own tents and bed. I stood outside a bit before going in my own tent. The night was beautiful, warm, and wet. A fitting end to a nice, pleasant little adventure.

On the road back from Lonesome Dove, there were signs of departure everywhere. Empty berms, cast-off sandbags, abandoned positions, and checkpoints falling apart.

Toward Al Mishab, on the Kuwaiti horizon, there was heavy, ominous, oily black smoke. Dense and dirty, the wind blowing it all south. A pall that covered the entire horizon. I had really never seen anything else like it. A huge forest fire, like the one whose smoke I saw hanging low over Carlsbad, can only approximate it.

As we drove, we were enveloped in smoke for 300 yards in every direction, which reminded me of Mordor in *The Lord of the Rings*. We passed bedouin encampments in the abandoned berms. There were white tents on green grass, dull white and bright white tents on the tender shoots of green grass that blanketed the earth, the desert floor, in this unseasonably wet and sun-blocked spring. Camels were grazing and lying down, the bedouins were going about their life in the midst of this checkered gloom as if nothing had changed or even interrupted the cycle of their existence. Seeing this made me think of how transitory all our efforts are. The berms are already being knocked down by the desert winds, and the bedouin have simply moved into what's left of them as if they were just another natural gift from their God to be wrested from the desert and used in their eternal struggle against it.

I saw my buses, too. The ones I had signed for at the port, the ones Hoss took north. They were stranded at the side of the road, abandoned and already rotting, like beached whales. There was also ammo, especially 155 shells, some lined up, some not, all along the side of the Al Mishab–Al Khanjar pipeline. Other ordnance, busted crates, and a load of laser guided missiles were scattered by the road.

26 March 1991

I worked on writing up awards today. Colonel Caldwell wants everybody in the S-3 to get at least a Navy Achievement Medal, and I'm cranking them out. I think today I was trying to do too many too fast. I have at least ten to do, and I did five today, but those five need considerable reworking. Major Stevenson says I need to say why something that was done was important, its significance, and Lieutenant Colonel Staunton tells me (without reading my write-ups, just as a general rule of thumb) that achievements should be above and beyond what is normally expected. So tomorrow I'll slow down a bit and beef up the awards.

I went to Wing today with Colonel Staunton. There was alot of talk about why the head honchos are just bolting and leaving stuff to be cleaned up and taken care of by the guys left behind. There are things that need to be addressed, things that need to be taken care of, like EAF matting, MPS gear, etc., but most of the bigwigs are just fluffing it off. They are going home.

People can get away with blowing things off. If they can get home, then whatever they needed to do will become the responsibility of somebody else, and they don't have to worry about it any longer or even concern themselves with its getting done. Then the people left behind are left with more and more things they have to take care of, more than they possibly can, and they begin to cut corners to take care of it all. And why shouldn't they? Why should they get jammed with this stuff rather than those who should be responsible for it? And that is when you start getting vehicles buried, abandoned equipment and supplies, wasted assets, and all the other horrors of waste, fraud, and abuse that happen when an army pulls up stakes and heads home. If the Chinese wanted to capture any of our equipment at Chosin, they shouldn't have fought us for it, they should have just surrendered and waited for us to pull out, then they could have had anything they wanted.

And why does this happen? Because commanders focus too much of their attention up instead of down. They want so badly to do what their own commander wants that they often don't take enough interest in making sure that what their own people need to have done is taken care of. Every commander should be fully responsible for embarking his unit in and out of a theater of operations, right up and down the chain of command. That way commanders would take along less and make sure whatever they took was properly accounted for and brought home. As things stand now, the logistics people are responsible for getting stuff home, and most commanding officers feel no compunction about leaving them behind to get it done. But when the CO leaves, the logistician's job becomes a nightmare. Without that command directive, people start disappearing, ship space goes to other units, and the focus of effort gets turned to other matters. At best the redeployment phase becomes an exercise in crisis management instead of a smooth, effective reconsolidation and redeployment of assets.

And who is finally to blame for this? The commanding officers, who just don't give a shit what happens to their stuff. No wonder everybody is always accusing us of being fat and of fighting with way too much stuff. How do you fight lean if nobody is ever responsible for keeping things trim in the first place?

Tony says FSSG/Port Ops are a mess. Stuff and personnel are everywhere. Is this to be expected? Is he exaggerating? Is this the way it always is? Or are they really having trouble? All through this war people have been complaining about FSSG support, and maybe, as with everything else they have done, the FSSG is having real trouble with this.

FSSG was asking for radios today. They brought over three Saber 1's to reprogram earlier, and a lieutenant came by requesting radios from us this evening. Colonel Coop is loving it.

Lightning storms tonight, and a little rain. Easter is this weekend. I thought of Maryanne picking me up at the BWI Airport after the San Diego Crew Classic one Easter so many years ago. Man, I miss her and want just to go home and be with her. Tomorrow is my birthday.

27 March 1991

My birthday today. I'm twenty-six years old. It's 2300 right now, and the camp is quiet. Kevin and I just got back from a buying trip out in Jubail City, and writing this is a nice close to a good day.

Being out in town, meeting with the vendors, Sallah, from the Sudan, and seeing the lights and shops of Jubail reminded me of how much of life there still is to see, know, and experience. In a multitude of lifetimes, a person couldn't cover all that he or she wants to learn and accomplish. Thinking of Africa, Spain, the Himalayas, Asia, Russia, books, ideas ... the list is endless. The sheer magnitude of it all makes you feel alive. It's frustrating to realize how little I'll be able to do in terms of experiencing everything and how many countries I'll never set foot in. But at the same time, the simple prospect of even trying to do it all sends a charge of life and living through me that connects me in some way with even those things I'll never be able to experience or do.

It's wonderful to be alive, to be young, to have the whole world ahead of you. I think the years ahead will be wonderful years. I must make the best of them and never take them for granted. Happy Birthday! And goodnight Maryanne, I love you.

28 March 1991

Went to Dahran with Major Howard and Dan White today. Then I played volleyball and got the crap knocked out of me by Sgt. Wall as he was trying to get an out-of-bounds ball. He basically ran over me trying to get it and somehow slammed into my bad leg. Now it's stiff and sore, and I can barely walk on it, let alone play volleyball. Guess I'll have to take a break from the volleyball games for a while.

Watched *Coming to America* tonight and then caught the tail end of General Schwarzkopf being interviewed by David Frost. The general is truly a remarkable, inspiring man, and I can understand now how soldiers feel about certain generals they have fought under. I'm proud to have fought under him and grateful for the job he did leading us.

They listed the names of our dead at the end of the program, against the Statue of Liberty, while the National Anthem played in the background. Don't ever forget these people and all the others like them throughout our history. Living the way we do is a privilege that has never come cheaply.

29 March 1991

Today I went looking for James at the port with Top Riley and John Clark and found out he had already left for home on the 27th. All right James. Then we headed down to Ras Al Gar to find Rick. He was up at IMEF when I finally found his unit's location, so I left a note for him at his tent and went to find Marc at his arty battalion. Wrong battalion, so off I went to rejoin John and Top Riley, who were walking around Ras Al Gar port taking it easy while I was out chasing these guys down.

I found them on the pier, and we headed down toward the end of it, about three and a half miles, where we could look off into the Arabian Gulf. It was beautiful out there. The water was opaque green, and bright fish were swimming here and there around the rocks. It was a beautiful, sunny day, and the white, completely empty beaches stretched as far as you could see. At the beach end of the pier, Marines were swimming, playing volleyball, picnicking, sailing, sunbathing, fishing, and playing in the water. They were all tankers, grunts, or artillerymen, all just taking it easy. This was an R and R spot for the

Division, and each unit that was bivouacked out here was taking full advantage of it, as well they should.

On the way out, we passed two helos setting down in the middle of the camp on the asphalt of a huge parking lot, debarking a squad of infantrymen. They looked bad: packs, rifles, helmets, goggles, with one or two acting the badass with their 60s and M-16s, as usual. Some things never change.

The rest of the day was easy and uneventful. I received four letters and wrote four. Played some volleyball.

Got word earlier that six Marines were wounded in a drive-by shooting outside Camp 3. I wonder, do we need our weapons back? Did we turn them in to soon? This is a perfect opportunity for terrorists to polarize U.S. and Saudi relations, which so far have been so good. The U.S. needs to decide what to do politically in this region and then get the hell out of here as soon as possible to prevent problems like this becoming serious. Tony wants his pistol back.

General Moore is gone (3D MAW CG), Colonel Levine is gone (3D MAW G-4) and most of the big brass have already left for the States. Awful nice of them.

30 March 1991

Duty tonight and a call home to my mother. As usual I had to let it ring a number of times before she answered, but when she did she sounded so happy to hear from me and immediately had a hundred things to tell me. I guess New England is getting hit really hard in this recession, and things at home are getting much tougher than they used to be.

Chapter 5
April

3 April 1991

We got word today that we might be leaving on the 20th, and all of a sudden everybody exploded in a flurry of activity. It was getting so depressing, doing nothing every day, and no real word of when we were getting out of here, that this new word really got people excited.

To keep occupied, I take boondoggle trips down to Ras Al Gar, hoping to see Rick, Dave, or Kerry, or I drive up to Camp 3, or anyplace for that matter, with Kevin or Sgt McEntire, or anybody else who is going anywhere. Last night I went down to Dammam with Kevin Roberts, Ryan Straus, Norville, Gareth, and Smith. We cruised around town, looked for trinkets, and basically just blew off a little steam. Yesterday seemed so depressing. This place is really getting old.

The trouble is not being able to get on with your life. We can't really make any plans or set any kind of personal goals because we have no control over what is going on here. You always end up frustrated and disappointed when nothing happens the way you want it to. I guess it is just a state of mind we will have to get used to. You have to go with the flow, not expect anything, not hope for anything, and just live day to day. Letting everything just sort of take care of itself. Then the days drift by, you don't get too excited about anything, and it all seems to go along the way it should.

I bought Maryanne a veil in Dammam and can't wait to see her wearing it. Hope she and all the rest of my family is doing okay and that I will be home with them all again soon.

5 April 1991

It's getting harder and harder to keep up with the journal. Everything is starting to drag so much around here that you just don't feel like doing anything. Seems as if everybody is getting on edge because of it too.

We had a class today on the readjustment process. Nothing like what the Vietnam vets or any of the other vets in past wars had to go through, but they gave us some good tips about what to expect, and overall it was a very good class. Really it was more like an end-of-the-deployment class — what to expect from family and friends, from your spouse, from yourself, etc. They pretty much told us that the depression we are feeling right now is just the result of the anxiety and complete uncertainty we are faced with about when we are going home and what the future will hold. That it is perfectly normal and not to get too worked up about it.

The instructor, a lieutenant colonel, spoke of depression as a state where you feel like doing nothing, even things you normally enjoy, and experience an inability to concentrate. This sounded like a perfect description of our volleyball game the other day. Everybody was so listless, not going after the ball if it was more than a few feet away and not even caring if we hit it or not.

He also spoke about life structure and flux. War, he said, is a period when you no longer have a normal routine to live within. You no longer just do the jobs you are expected to. Nothing is steady and going back to a peacetime environment is difficult because you go back to a state of order and limitations.

This made me think of James Webb's *Fields of Fire*. Maybe the city kid was good at his job and fit in there because his whole life up to that point had been one of unstructured day-to-day existence. He had found his niche and a lifestyle that sanctioned the way he lived normally. And the kid from the upper-middle-class background had trouble because his life had been based on order, reason, and a discernable pattern, of which there is little in war. You really do have to be able to flow with life in these situations. You should be thinking from meal to meal, from one activity to the next, and grabbing rest in between times as well as you can by relaxing yourself and not stressing out over the seeming randomness of it all.

I think that is why a school like BUDS might be easier for a combat vet than it would be for a regular new candidate because the vet knows what is important and what isn't. He doesn't think too far ahead of himself and just doesn't get worked up about everything as a new candidate is apt to do.

Live moment to moment. Make no plans and have no expectations. Just exist.

Funny that in peacetime it is the exact opposite kind of existence that gets you ahead. And that is what the best parents leave their children — a sense of the rules, of order, of what it takes to get ahead and how to get there.

Later I decided to go ahead and begin the embarkation process on the

Motorola radio equipment I'm responsible for. As usual the first stop I made was with LCpl. Danielson and Lance Cpl. Puck, who were already putting boxes together to get stuff out of here. (Funny how you always see the same guys working hard and getting things done. These were two of the best.) They gave me pointers on how to make a frame around a large piece of gear, like the repeater, to get it shipped out.

After a bit of scrounging, I came up with the wood I needed to make the frame and did my best to do exactly as Danielson and Puck showed me earlier. Needless to say it didn't look quite like what they had described or what I had hoped for. Tony laughed his ass off when he saw it but said he thought it would be good enough to protect the repeater when we shipped it out. To cover this eyesore, I found a big cardboard box that I could fit over the repeater and the frame and jammed it on. Finally it looked good to go. I thought I would save a picture of the frame for embark school back home, to show them what a fine job they had done teaching proper embarkation procedures to new lieutenants, but I was too lazy to take the cardboard box back off.

Patience is the key to all this stuff. You have to take the time to do it right and know what the hell you are doing. I am learning embark though, which I should know already, being an 04 and all. Tomorrow I will get the stenciling done and begin loading up the pallet. Tony already got me the pallet and ropes, and I got all the boxes I'll need. If we have to, we can jam the boxes down to the proper height with forklift prongs, which is the unofficial, best way to meet the 96" height limitation. If this seems like the "flying by the seat of your pants" type of embarkation, it is, but there are reasons for that.

7 April 1991

Tomorrow the first group of the main body leaves for home. As I hoped, the movement of us back to the States is going quicker than originally planned. We just don't need all these people over here, so many of them are getting sent home. And today all the showers have the stall doors back on, so you can take a shower in privacy again. The Saudi mess is also going full swing. I don't think MWSS-174 Food Services has to do any of the meals any more, which means that another of our services here has been shut down, and our hour of departure is probably drawing closer. Things are definitely happening. The question now is, when us?

I just can't believe we will actually go home at some point. I get homesick, but I think I have buried any real hope of going home to avoid the disappointment of it not happening. Funny, I wonder how much of our lives we spend waiting and rushing to get to the next point, never really living in the present. And before you know it, your whole life is past. So live in the present. But I still want to see my wife.

Spent yesterday embarking the S-3 shop for sea lift. I keep wanting to get it all ready to go, but everybody else doesn't have that same sense of urgency. Today I staged the Motorola equipment for airlift. More volleyball. Our last game? Still, it's really hard to get into it. Felt so unresponsive.

As usual the move out of here is going along fitfully. There is lots of radio traffic over the Motorolas, with everybody listening in on everybody else's screwups. Our mistakes, 3D MAW's, FSSG's, MAG-13's, etc. Set right out there for all the world to hear. Bungled departure times, embarkation screwups, arrival time screwups, leap-exs for units getting out of here, only to learn later at the airport that their plane is already filled, transportation problems on the ground, all sorts of stuff. Listening to it makes you wonder if we will ever get out of here.

8 April 1991

The first really large group of people left today to go home. Jerry Healey, Top Riley, Gunney Hendrix, Cpl. Scott and Sgt. Bose. I'd told everybody that they would be responsible for embarking whatever gear they were accountable for before they left and for cleaning up their office spaces and living areas. Everybody did a pretty good job of it, with one or two exceptions, of course.

With Hendrix and Riley gone, there were other things that popped up which still needed to be taken care of. Their jobs got dumped in the lap of SSgt. James, whose wife is due soon back home, and Gunney Pescatore. Gunney Hendrix left a bunch of trucks out on the back lot which still need to be turned into the port. Almost all of them are deadlined, and it has fallen to James and Pescatore to get the job done.

Colonel Caldwell also wants us to get more trucks from somewhere to help move MWSS-271 south to Shaikh Isa. Before they can get out of here, SSgt. James and Gunney Pescatore have to get both of these assignments finished.

The colonel had the entire Group headquarters called together today for the last time to tell us all goodbye. He thanked us for the job we had done and congratulated us on the results of our hard work and outstanding efforts on behalf of the 3D MAW. He is a good man and a good leader. He spoke calmly, seriously, and with great dignity, but he is not too stiff and is perfectly able to put any of us at ease. I thought a lot about this and about Colonel Caldwell and Colonel Staunton, and how effective each of them was in leading us and getting the MWSG-37 mission accomplished.

I think all three of them possess that same sense of calm and control that is so important in getting things taken care of and keeping everybody from getting all worked up. If I have judged any of them too harshly at times, I have to remember what the end result was of all they have managed to do over here. We got the mission accomplished, and we're going home with everybody we came over with. What more could you ever hope for, in even the best of circumstances.

The sky was heavy with the black clouds from Kuwait and a sprinkle of rain. We played a few last games of volleyball, said our goodbyes, and those who were leaving headed out.

Now we will just sit and wait for the next group to go, and I'll say to myself every day, just to make sure I don't get my hopes up, "We're never getting out of here." And I'll say this every day until the day we do.

12 April 1991

Another day drifting by. Still depressed, still so hard to get into doing anything. Read a bit today, played a little Risk, wrote some, ate, watched a few movies, and now I'm hitting the sack. Not much of a life. We keep getting different word on when we will be going home. The journal is getting hard to keep up because I'm just not into it as much as I was before. Seems as if I'm blah about everything now, especially anything which demands concentration, like writing. It's just too hard to get up for.

The one bright spot of the day today was talking to Maryanne. Please God, keep her safe.

16 April 1991

Another day gone, like all the rest. We wake up at 0600. Kevin and I PT, maybe go for a run and do a few calisthenics, or just go for a run. Hit the showers, which are much less crowded now. Eat. Go to work. Clean up a little. Read. Eat lunch. Play one or two games of Risk. Eat dinner, watch some movies, and then go to bed again. Each day like the last, boring and uneventful.

Still, people are getting out of here. They keep disappearing. Here one day, gone the next. SSgt. James is finally gone, and more and more people seem to be going every day. The soccer stadium is beginning to look more open and more like a regular soccer stadium every day. The change is extraordinary from what this place looked like only a few weeks ago and never ceases to amaze me.

The rest of us feel as if we are getting nowhere. Kevin is depressed, I'm depressed, even Hoss is depressed. We are just sick of it here.

The Group headquarter's comm is shut down, and now all we have left communicationwise are our three civilian line phones. We are also doing our best to shut down the rest of the camp and get it embarked for home. Tomorrow four more tents go down, and maybe the last repeater in the stadium. MWSS-174 utilities arrive in the morning, then construction, then we inspect the troops and ship them out.

Joe was up today. His men screwed him over getting their MPS gear ready for reembarkation on the MPS ships. His "D" TAMS didn't pass, and now they have to do it all over again. Poor Joe, he's had enough of this place too and they are already telling him he might be staying on after everybody else leaves. He just doesn't have anybody looking out for him down there, and that fucking squadron is going to jam him.

I don't know why I'm still so depressed about it all. May 3-9 has always been the date I was to go home, with a few false alarms about it being earlier, but I keep thinking I will get out of here sooner. I don't even know why I think about it. It will happen when it happens. SSgt. Heath says you have to live where you are and quit wishing you were someplace else. Good advice if I have ever heard any, and he ought to know. He has been in the Marine Corps long enough to get that down pat.

17 April 1991

Another group of people left today. Capt. O'Brien, Sgt. Wall, Saks, Danielson, Noonan, Snipes, Whitaker, etc. In the morning, Kevin and I had them tear down the tents they were leaving, in the early afternoon we inspected their gear, and we finally saw them off at about 1725. When they were gone, Kevin thought we would move our own stuff from the tent we were staying in to one of the last enlisted tents still up, so we could tear down the officers' tent. But the enlisted tent was a pig pen, with wood partitions nailed up everywhere to section off each space, which made the whole tent as dark and hot as all get out, so we decided to move into the headquarters buildings instead.

This turned out to be a great idea. There were so few of us left that we could fit about two to a room, and even though the chow hall and showers are a bit farther away, living like this is much easier than living in the tents. It's almost like being back in college, and Kevin and I can sit up half the night shooting the shit, relaxing and listening to music whenever we feel like it. And we have no problem keeping the room neat, organized, and relatively clean. Now still being out here doesn't seem all that bad.

Kevin got almost everybody else left to move out to the headquarters buildings as well, so now he will have no problem breaking down the last of the tents still standing in the parking lot. Sgt. McEntire has her own room. Dan has his own room. Tony has his. Lisa is sharing one with one of the female Marines who works for her. Marquez has his own room, etc. I think Colonel Caldwell is still living out of his tent, but he is about the only one.

About the only thing I have to watch is Warrant Officer Radell, who is hanging around the female Marines. Every time I'm over in the S-3, he seems to be hanging around their rooms talking. He would probably be the first to complain about women not having a place in the Marine Corps, and you know it's always guys like that who can never get enough of trying to put the moves on the WMs whenever they get the chance.

Went on a run to IMEF and a few other places with Kevin earlier today. Out in town, and especially out in front of the IMEF headquarters buildings, with the freshly bloomed flowers, the faintly warm day, and the clean air, I thought about how much this all reminded me of a summer's day back in New England. It will be good to go home.

18 April 1991

I'm going over the edge with this embark stuff. I keep wanting things to happen faster and with a greater sense of personal responsibility. Getting things organized, packed up or thrown away, and generally taken care of seems important, but it's hard to get done. Seems as if few people have any interest in cleaning up after themselves. They use an office space or live in a certain area in a certain tent, and when it is their turn to go home, they just pack up their stuff and leave. They don't clean up their trash. They don't throw away any of their garbage or the things they have scrounged up to make their lives more comfortable over here. They just leave. It's bad enough that they don't think to clean up after themselves. It smacks of something even worse if they expect the rest of us left behind to do it all, which is almost without exception what is happening.

And if this goes on at our own small level, how much worse is it at higher levels where you have people leaving with major jobs undone. It just doesn't seem as if people are being held accountable for what they are responsible for. There is just no command interest in redeployment. If there was and there was "no going home until the job is done" type thinking going on, you can bet all this would get done and get done right. But that doesn't happen, and things just keep getting passed off to whoever is left in country. It becomes their responsibility to embark everything that is left behind, no matter who originally owned it or where it came from.

And what do these guys do? You can't embark everything because you simply don't have the people to do it. It took everybody involved to get the stuff over here in the first place. How do they expect to get it all back properly with only one-fourth of that number, at best? So you get rid of it the best you can. I'm throwing out food, tarps, tents, cots, rolls of banding wire, and anything else I can't take care of. Maybe if somebody cared about this stuff and getting it out of here, I wouldn't have to just waste it all, but they don't, so why should I?

If every person was responsible up and down the chain of command for getting their own shop in order, getting it in and out in as orderly and efficient manner as possible, then deployments and redeployments would work much more smoothly. Much less stuff would go to waste, and we would make better use of valuable assets. It's the same thing they teach you in boot camp — take care of your stuff and keep it organized. I wonder why that gets so completely washed out of our thinking along the way.

Kevin is like I am. He hates disorganization and clutter. He hates not having things taken care of and finished off. "Better to do it yourself and do it right then to try and get everybody else fired up about it when they just don't give a shit" is what he is always saying. So we spend almost all of our time now breaking down the hardback tents with the MWSS-174 construction and utility guys and Lisa's MPs and then cleaning up all the trash that everybody else has left behind, like beds, homemade furniture, rags, magazines, etc. And that is only in the living spaces. In the work spaces, we still have tools to take care of, typewriters, paper, copier machines, computers and printers, desks, you name it.

But I let this stuff get to me. Who cares? So stuff gets trashed, so we throw a lot of gear out that we might be able to use again. Maybe the work and bother of getting it home and the cost isn't worth it anyway.

"Man, you got to relax," Kevin keeps telling me. And he is right. There is no need to get worked up about all this. I guess it's what happens in any war.

There are not many of us left now. Maybe about twenty out of the whole Group headquarters. Colonel Coop, Colonel Caldwell, Major Stevenson, Major Howard, Major Bacall, Captain Morrison, Kevin, Coleman, Tony, Dan, Richard, me, Gunney Pescatore, SSgt. Heath, Sgt. Pepper, Sgt. McEntire, Hall, Marquez, and a few others. But that is about it, besides Lisa and her MPs.

20 April 1991

Almost everybody is gone now. Major Howard left yesterday — his wife just had a baby girl back home. Coleman Brady leaves this morning. Lieutenant Dean, Gunney Pescatore, and the MPs left this morning. And Richard, Hall, Henry, and SSgt. Pepper finally got a plane for their pallet and are leaving tomorrow morning. The whole place is almost shut down.

And as usual, there is still a lot left to do. All the banding wire has to be taken care of for a start.

The banding wire story is a pretty good one. Coleman figured they would need a considerable amount of banding wire to get the AM-2 matting out of Lonesome Dove and to the port at Al Mishab. Then when they were there, they needed to unband it to hose it down for shipment back to the United States on container ships. The AM-2 matting has to go home because it is so valuable and expensive to replace, and it has to have all the sand and grit cleaned off it before it goes so it doesn't get ruined on the way.

To band up AM-2 matting, you stack about ten sheets on top of each other and then band it all together as you would any other embarkation package. The sheets of matting are extremely heavy and very unwieldy if they aren't bound tight enough, so you need pretty strong banding wire to keep them together.

And the banding wire itself is unbelievably heavy. It comes in a large roll, and it is high quality metal, so a load of the stuff can get pretty heavy, to say the least.

Anyway, for a long time all Coleman talked about was banding wire. He swore that MWSS-273 didn't have enough to get all the AM-2 matting out of Lonesome Dove, and he thought nobody was taking the proper interest in getting what they needed to have it done. So he goes to Major Howard and tells him he needs at least 1800 rolls of banding wire ASAP if MWSS-273 is going to get itself out of Lonesome Dove anytime soon. Major Howard got Colonel Coop to buy off on pushing the order, and before you know it. word was on the streets that MWSG-37 needed banding wire and needed it fast.

From early April on, MWSG-37 had been pushing to get this stuff, but it just wasn't coming in fast enough for Major Howard or Coleman. Major Howard started thinking the FSSG was blowing him off on it, and Coleman was getting more desperate to have the stuff every day.

So Major Howard made a big stink about not getting support from the FSSG and highlighted the people who were trying to get the banding wire for us there, jumped the supply line to order it directly from the United States, and also ordered it outside the system to make sure that we at least got it from somewhere as soon as possible.

Then all the orders went through, and our precious banding wire started coming in, just as we had asked. We got our 1800 rolls of it and staged it behind the headquarters buildings. And it still kept coming. We had 2000, 3000, 4000 rolls, and every day trucks were bringing in more. I don't know where they got it all, but it just kept coming.

Coleman didn't need that much and separated his 1800 rolls from the rest, which should have been sent back. But nobody sent it back. That would have meant a loss of face. We had raised such a stink about the stuff that to send it back would have made us look like fools. So it just sat there. I don't know what people expected would happen with the stuff— sooner or later we would have to take care of it.

Then Coleman left and Major Howard soon after him. And still the banding wire just sat there, even Coleman's 1800 rolls, which he had separated from the rest of the banding wire and staged separately. I guess MWSS-273 managed to make do without the stuff after all. Not that it would have done them any good anyway, because there were no clips and no banding tools to go along with it.

Now who is stuck with getting rid of all this stuff? Why the lieutenants, of course. The basic problem with us getting all this banding wire is the same problem we have had the whole time over here. We definitely tend to overmanage, even micromanage, the support squadrons underneath us. Instead of having MWSS-273 tell us what they actually needed to get the matting moved out of Lonesome Dove, Coleman estimated the requirements himself, thinking they weren't on top of the situation enough to do it on their own. Just before he left, we were all helping him box up a bunch of lighting gear he had staged out on the road in front of our headquarters. When I asked him why Group had all this stuff and not the support squadrons, who actually used it, he told me he didn't trust them enough to take care of it.

It was no better dealing with all the equipment the support squadrons brought over here and the other stuff they received off the MPS ships. In some cases we gave an entire squadron's heavy equipment and motor transport assets, which they had embarked themselves from the States, to another support squadron. Then we would fill out the support squadron whose gear we had given away with other stuff as it came in. Naturally this didn't make us many friends on the support squadron side, and I'm sure if you asked the support squadrons what their impressions were of Group's performance over here, you would get a very different answer than you would if you asked any of us.

So Coleman goes high and to the left and orders all this banding wire without checking with the support squadron that supposedly needs it to make sure they actually do. But that is okay because many times you do need to estimate support requirements and plan for eventual contingencies. That is the way potential problems are avoided later on. What a staff does is think of as many things as possible that can go wrong and continually work to highlight every potential consideration in an operation so it all goes off smoothly when it needs to. And sometimes you make mistakes, but it is always better to have something and not need it than to not have it and run the risk of it being a very important requirement later on.

Then Major Howard made his contribution to the banding wire bonanza. He was trying to do what he thought was the right thing by ordering the banding material from as many places as possible and raising such a big stink over it to make sure it came in. If it was as important as Coleman made it out to be, then we definitely needed it, and Major Howard was going to make sure we had it. But he was thinking too much like a supply officer, which is what he has always been in the past and what his MOS is, and not enough like a logistics officer, which is what he is acting as now in the MWSG-37 S-4 billet.

A supply officer will move heaven and earth to get his people what they need. It's what they pride themselves on. It's what they do. But a logistics officer does a little more than just fill every order he is asked to meet. It's his responsibility to determine the requirements of that order, to make sure that it is filling a real need. Supply lines are vital in any conflict, and trying to jam too much through them is just as bad as not getting enough through and being short of stuff. The end result is the same. In either case the system works at a slower pace and important requirements get lost in the log jam. This happened to the U.S. Army during the Normandy breakout in World War II, and ever since then military strategists have been very sensitive to the need to keep supply lines fast, efficient, and responsive. A logistics officer's job is to make this happen the best he can at whatever level he is operating on. It is his responsibility to make sure the system doesn't get bogged down with unnecessary or unreal requirements.

You have to talk to the people asking for the stuff, determine if it is really as high priority as they think, and then act accordingly. A great logistics officer will estimate many of requirements in advance to get the supply chain really working for him, but there will always be those times when something else comes up that is a high priority and needs to come in fast. And the supply chain should be set up to make that happen.

Major Howard didn't really do this. He just ordered what he was told to order and made sure we would get it. Again this is better than the alternative of needing something and not having it, and mistakes are going to be made in the war business. So in that sense he really didn't do anything wrong. The mistake was in not taking care of the problem when it was obvious that it was a problem. We have had about a million dollars worth of banding wire just sitting out back for about a month now, and nobody has done a thing to take care of it. Like everything else, it just got blown off and ignored, as though it was going to take care of itself, and eventually the problem will be passed on to whoever is last to leave.

Kevin and I joke about this all the time because we knew it would come down to this. Making fun of it is a way of blowing off steam, and it definitely works. Writing this journal is a way of blowing off steam. Both of us like to see things finished off properly, with all the loose ends tied up the way they should be. Over here that never happens, nothing ever seems completely finished, and it will drive you crazy if you let it. I'm even starting to dream about cleaning, getting things packed up, organized, and moving out of here. And I can see this happening to Kevin, too. We are becoming obsessed with embarkation, neatness, and organization.

Oh well, a good leader knows how to block this stuff out, to handle only what is important. Think of getting it done. We have got to move the banding wire out of here and clean up the rest of the camp. Kevin has got to close out his BPA authority, and I have to get all the Motorola stuff home. Period.

21 April 1991

I've been pretty sick lately. I think I must have picked it up from Kevin, whatever it is, because he was real sick a few days ago and is just getting over it. After our run and calisthenics two days ago, I got a runny nose that quickly turned into a pretty heavy duty cold. Yesterday and today I've been fighting it, taking Dextoral and basically sleeping all day. Now finally I think I'm getting over it. It's probably all the worrying that really took it out of me. I'm always getting headaches and colds whenever I go through any big move or change, and here we are responsible for closing down the base. No wonder I feel so whacked out.

Colonel Caldwell said to stage the banding wire at Jubail Airport so anybody who needs it can use it. As usual he is taking all this in stride, to him it's no big deal. That is the right way to handle it.

Portions of food at the chow hall are getting huge. Arab caterers do every meal we have now, which is breakfast and dinner. When they first started doing it about two weeks ago, they gave us hardly anything for portions, maybe one meat portion and a small scoop of vegetables, etc. I don't know if they thought we didn't eat that much, or they didn't have the food because there were more people here then and they needed to stretch what they had. Now they are giving us food out the ying-yang.

Kevin got three burger patties tonight, and the guy wanted to know if he wanted more. And that is nothing compared to what they give you on the side. I had my plate out for the food and looked away for a moment, and when I looked back I had three heaping spoonfuls of rice on my plate, way more than I could possibly eat. And the guy who was serving me was dishing out more. "You want more? More cucumber? Tomatoes?" The number of people left here has really dwindled, which means they probably have more food now than they know what to do with.

Spent most of today cruising around Jubail and Dammam with Kevin, sleeping in the car while he got his work done with the shops and vendors for whom he still had BPA accounts. Guess I was pretty knocked out from the Dextoral.

Kevin ended up getting hardly anything done, just ran around getting more and more frustrated. He couldn't get the Honda fixed or the accident claim on it straightened out as he thought he would be able to do today, and the JVC camera he had brought in to get fixed still wasn't ready, only the VCR was. We did get to eat at the Pizza Sheikh and had some ice cream at Baskin Robbins. That definitely made the day much more cheery. Still, this place is getting old. When are we getting out of here?

22 April 1991

Got a lot of work done today. I pulled a cheap one on MWSS-273, and now they are the proud owners of almost all our banding wire, which is staged who knows where up at Jubail Airport.

We had a bunch of trucks staged out back that were going to MWSS-273. Yesterday Colonel Caldwell gave them a call and told them to send down drivers to pick up the trucks sometime today. So this morning I got MWSS-174 to send over a TRAM, which is a big forklift, and begin loading the banding wire onto the trucks. That way when the MWSS-273 drivers arrived to pick up the trucks the banding wire would already be loaded and ready to go, and all of it would get hauled to the airport whether they were ready for it or not.

But this stuff was heavy. Way heavier than I thought it was. I tried loading too much of it on the first tractor trailer and ended up blowing the back two tires out. After this, we spaced the rolls out evenly along the bed of the truck and left plenty of room between the bundles. We got about 35 bundles of the banding wire loaded before we ran out of truck space. This meant I would have to get the MWSS-273 drivers to bring the trucks back for a second run, which was another nice thing for me to pull on them, considering they had no idea they were even hauling the banding wire in the first place. They thought they were coming down to Group to pick up some trucks we had borrowed from them and hadn't returned, and I'm boning them into making runs for us they don't even know about. A typical Group-style operation.

When the drivers arrived, I filled them in on what was going on. They were really good about it and took it all in stride. To them it was just another day, just another run, and just some other job that needed to be taken care of.

On their way out, one of the trucks dumped its load when it got stuck in the ditch at the end of the road. The TRAM got the truck out, and I told them to write off the banding wire. We had more than enough left to take care of, and whenever the rolls came loose they were just too big a pain in the ass to bother with. Once the trucks were gone the TRAM driver speared the rolls of unwound banding wire in the ditch the best he could, and I had him dump the stuff in the trash heap out in back of our headquarters. If anybody wanted it, they were welcome to it.

They left one truck behind that I was going to use for the conex box. To load it I needed a RTCH, which is a huge piece of heavy equipment used to pick up containers. The one that MWSS-174 had was already gone, so I went across the street to the civilian contractors who had come in to load up all the Marine Corps Aviation yellow gear. Yellow gear is flight line equipment used by the Marine Corps that really isn't part of the Marine Corps supply system. It is purchased from government vendors for flight line use, but it really isn't military. The civilians taking care of it had come on board about a week ago and were responsible for getting it all loaded up and taken care of so the Marines could go home. The civilians stayed at one of the camps nearer Jubail Airport, but they worked at King Abdul Aziz Naval Base every day.

I went over there and asked them if they would let me use a RTCH and operator for a bit, and they were happy to comply. The guys who helped me out were pretty cool. They knocked off what they were doing and let me take them right to where the conex box was across the street.

I told them the box was probably pretty heavy and that the RTCH might not be able to lift it, but they said not to worry, that they had never known any box or container the RTCH hadn't been able to lift. They drove up, maneuvered the RTCH into the proper position, hooked her up, and started lifting, but the conex box didn't move, the RTCH did. Its back end came right up off the sand. The two guys couldn't believe it. The RTCH's limit is about 50,000 pounds, so the box had to weigh more than that.

It was somebody's bright idea to jam the conex box full of as much banding wire as it could take, then get it embarked aboard one of the ships at the port so we would get it back to the States. Needless to say this wasn't going to work.

Marquez spent the rest of the day dragging the bundles of banding wire out of the conex box. It was long, tedious work. He had to hook the bottom of the pallets the bundles were on with the prongs of the 4000 forklift and then drag them out slowly. Some of the bundles had fallen over. We had to hook these up to the towing cable at the back of the forklift and drag them out that way. Marquez did a great job. The hard part for him was maneuvering the forklift around the inside of the conex box to get all the banding wire out. It took time, but he did it.

We were fighting to finish before nightfall. Marquez finished about thirty minutes after dark by the light of his headlamps. Then he went back to work typing up reports for Major Bacall, who chewed him out for doing all the work for me with the banding wire and neglecting his job with her.

I hope I can get the rest of this stuff out of here tomorrow.

23 April 1991

Major Bacall, Dan, Marquez, McEntire, SSgt. Heath, and the corpsman took the day off and went down to Bahrain today for a change of pace and a little relaxation. They hooked up with Major Stevenson, who is down at MWSS-373, and spent the day touring the shops, sightseeing, and downing a few cold ones. Bahrain is about the only place you can drink around here, so almost everybody heads down there when they get time off.

I keep trying to convince Kevin to go to Riyadh with me, but he has been too busy to get away. We had better get there sooner or later. I'll be bummed if I leave Saudi Arabia without seeing Riyadh.

I got the rest of the banding wire out of here today. Kevin and I were joking about sending a note on the conex box to Major Conrad, "To Cricket," which is his call sign, because both of us know how badly we are shafting these guys with this stuff. Might as well be honest about it. What the hell Major Conrad or Major Osborn are going to do with all the banding wire and no tools or clips to go with it is anybody's guess. It will probably just sit up at the airport until we all get out of here and then disappear into the sand. I thought we might as well just have had the trucks that delivered it all unload it into the ocean. We could have staged it there and not worried about it.

I learned how to drive a 4000 today. Marquez showed me in the morning, and I spent the day cleaning up the area where all the banding had been. I drove to the dump whatever was leftover after the tractor trailers departed and then picked up whatever other trash was lying around. The place looks pretty good now. It's weird that it all looks so empty. From the headquarters I can see right to the bank overlooking the water. Only a month ago my view would have been blocked by tents, equipment, containers, fences, everything that goes along with an encamped airfield. Today there is nothing left of all that. Just sand.

And the concrete foundations we had the tents on. Kevin and I are immortalized forever, or at least as long as the spray paint lasts, on one of them. It says, "Quickdraw and Kokes, Team Motorola." Snipes did that before he left.

I also spent much of the day running around trying to get a part on the repeater fixed. Jim Flobeck showed up this morning with the rest of his radios and the last of the repeaters we had had in the stadium, which means Okie can't talk to Zeke anymore from the airport. We tried putting it up at the headquarters, and Jim busted his ass getting it installed because we were leaving at 1800, but he didn't have time to help me fix one of the parts on it that had been broken when they took it down. So I spent the late afternoon chasing down the part I needed at El Maco and Comm Company. Finally I found a tech at Comm Company to help me out who knew what he was doing, and in about a half an hour I was on my way home.

I got back just in time to see the MWSS-174 buses pulling out. Jim, John, Jason, and all the rest of the guys were on their way home.

We hooked up the repeater, and I think it is working now, but we still can't get the airport. I think it's because the antenna is too low. Before it was on the roof of the stadium, now it is on the roof of the headquarters building. Colonel Caldwell wants it back on top of the stadium, but Major Hardy and Colonel Biotti told me the place is being shut down completely tomorrow, which means there will be no electricity and no reason even to try putting it back up. Guess we will just have to use the mobile unit hooked up in the colonel's car to talk to the airport.

Tonight is pretty quiet. The stadium is almost completely empty now and will be locked up tomorrow. Major Hardy let us have the key to the showers, so we can still get washed up, but we are on our own as far as meals go. We have plenty of MREs, tray packs, and frozen entree dinners to eat, and more than enough water to go along with it all, so we are more than comfortable. It's just weird to think we have been left here by ourselves and that we are just kind of camped out in the middle of nowhere.

The others got back from Bahrain a few hours ago and went almost straight to bed. They had obviously had a good time, and it was equally as obvious that they hadn't had a drink in about six months. Kevin is still working on getting his invoices done and tells me that tomorrow he is sure he will get rid of the BPA, finally, which he has been telling me about every day for the past week.

Tony is in his room tonight too, which is unusual. He spends almost all of his time at the port loading the ships, and he is about as happy as Kevin and I about still being here. Tony got shipped over here only a month after he had returned from an unaccompanied tour on Okinawa. He has also been at TBS and at Log School, since they yanked him out of the 03 field when they made him a warrant officer. In that whole time, he has probably seen his family for a total of about four weeks. His three-year-old son doesn't know him, and his six-year-old son thinks his parents might be divorced. "Are you divorced, Mom?" he asks.

The Marine Corps can be a hard place. A Marine Corps wife definitely earns the right to feel any way she wants about the Marine Corps. No wonder Tony gets so bitter and depressed sometimes.

He is also about to lose it up at the port. He has a hard enough time fighting to get his stuff loaded. Now I hear some major is riding him about getting a Land Rover loaded. Every general and full bird colonel over here wants his own personal Land Rover sent back to the States, and they are assigning majors and captains the task of getting them home. So Tony has to deal with these guys whining about not getting their Land Rovers and Toyotas embarked quickly enough. That one major in particular is a real pain in the ass.

I told Tony that if he wanted I would sneak up there and roll the thing off the pier and into the bay. He might take me up on it.

All of us are tired, irritable, and really getting on one another's nerves. Small things are becoming big things. I see this in the others and definitely see it in myself.

Some Arabs showed up today looking for their trucks. They had seen our carnival trucks loading up out back and thought we might know where to find theirs. It seems that all the trucks we have been using have been borrowed from individual Saudis, and now they are having a hard time getting them back because they are spread out all over the country. I told them how to get to the port, to Wing, and to IMEF. Maybe somewhere along the line somebody can help them out, but I doubt it. I would lay money on the fact that whoever was responsible for the trucks is already gone and that right now some poor fool is trying to figure out what units got what trucks and where they all went to without the slightest idea of where to even begin.

On their way out the Arabs thanked me, then told me that the motor transport coordinator they were used to dealing with was gone. He had already gone home to America.

24 April 1991

Talked to Maryanne today and only ended up more depressed than I was before. It's like I don't know her anymore. I feel as if she doesn't need me the way she used to, that she has made a life of her own and that she is completely independent of me. I always feel as if I'm growing closer to her during our separations. I think for her it's the opposite.

Always in the past when I've gone away for a while and come back, it takes her a few days to adjust and it really throws me because I remember her as the loving, devoted wife she was when I left. This is what it feels like now, only worse.

And I'm almost afraid to think about seeing her again because I just can't believe I will ever get out of here at some point and home. I feel so disinterested, so adrift, as though some sort of listless resignation has hold of me and I just can't shake it.

I guess that is why the jokes and the laughing are so important. Kevin and I make fun of everything now, nothing is sacred. If anybody could hear what we were saying, we would probably get in a lot of trouble about disrespect and our attitudes in general. But that is how we blow of steam. That and the journal.

The journal has become more than what it was when I started it. I don't feel as if I'm writing for just myself any longer, I feel I'm writing for an audience, so I'm trying to get down everything. Every event, every feeling, every action, every attitude; I want to get it all. I want to paint a picture of what it is like being over here. I also think of it as a kind of payback or a ledger of reckoning, where I can put down what happened over here, at least as I see it, without pulling any punches. I just have to keep it fair.

Maybe I'm just homesick and taking all this packing up too much to heart. After all, isn't it the job of logisticians, embarkers, and other personnel remaining behind to take care of it all? Naa.

They are responsible to see it gets done, but should definitely have help doing it. Good Marines don't just leave their own shit behind for other Marines to take care of.

25 April 1991

Getting the last pallet put together today. All the rest of the office equipment that is going home and my radios are on it. I'm waiting to close it up, but Colonel Caldwell still has a few messages to get out, so Sgt. McEntire and I can't completely break down the shop yet.

In the afternoon Kevin, Tony, and I went out into town for pizza and ice cream. All we do now to pass the time is bust on everybody — especially the losers who are already home.

We also had forklift races today. Tony and I got them revved up and ready to go, but when we started I took too sharp of a turn and blew a ball on the tire, flattening it right out. I felt pretty bad about it, but Tony just laughed. Ahh, messing up gear by fooling around on it, the usual story. Not that anybody is responsible for our forklifts now anyway. They are all extras Tony appropriated from somewhere, and when we leave we will give them all to the civilians across the street to use.

I also found out I am gear rider with SSgt. Heath on the last pallet, which means we will be the last people out of here from MWSG-37. Besides Colonel Coop, of course, who got tagged as the acting commanding officer for the 3D MAW when General Moore took off.

Tonight I collated all the radio information and updated it on the computer so I can brief Colonel Coop on it tomorrow. The rest of the guys are at the port helping Major Hardy get some of his last minute gear embarked on ships out of here. Some of the MAG-16 aviation fuel tanks weren't packed properly, and they are all up there now constructing new wooden crates, loading the tanks inside them, and then getting them banded up so the ships will accept them.

Tony, Kevin, Hoss, Marquez, and McEntire are up there now with Major Hardy getting this taken care of. Besides Major Hardy, none of them are from MAG-16, the unit that owns the fuel tanks, but they are still responsible for getting the job done because nobody else is here to do it.

28 April 1991

Yesterday all but three people of the MWSG-37 Headquarters left for home. Colonel Coop, Captain Morrison, and I are still here and will be the last to leave. Colonel Coop is the acting 3D MAW Commander, Captain Morrison stayed to see Kuwait and will ride back with me, and I got picked to ride the pallet back because of all the Motorola radio equipment that is on it.

I woke up yesterday in a foul mood and could barely speak to anybody because of my hurt, anger, confusion, and deep sense of impending loneliness. I felt as if I was being left behind. After a while I relaxed, and I saw them all off. Tony, Kevin, Hoss, Sgt. McEntire and all the rest of them, the people who had meant the most to me over here. All said warm goodbyes and then jumped aboard the 5-ton that would take them to the airport.

I felt like the sergeant at the end of *Platoon* waving goodbye as Charlie Sheen is flying away in the helo, except I had a broom instead of a rifle. I bid farewell to them all — Colonel Caldwell, Major Bacall, Major Stevenson, Warrant Officer Rominger, Warrant Officer Clark, Lieutenant Roberts, Lieutenant White, Staff Sergeant Heath, Sergeant McEntire, and Corporal Garcia Marquez. As I watched the 5-ton, it faded into the dust down the road.

Then I was alone. The last combat Marine at King Abdul Aziz Naval Base. I would be the one to turn off the lights, to lock up. Ironic, because only months earlier in the States I had seen a picture of the Marines at the Scud Bowl watching one of the women's football games that they used to play all the time on the field. All of them looked hard, bad, and motivated. I envied them because they were actually a part of what was going on, and you could see it in their faces, while I just sat at home. Now here I am, not hard, not bad, just lonely, and locking up those same gates.

I spent the morning packing my stuff, made my last few phone calls to Mom and Kerry, Ryan, and finally Maryanne, then took the phones down and loaded them in with the rest of the pallet. I buckled up the cargo netting over the pallet the best I could, with the corpsman's help, and then locked on transportation with MWSS-273 and brought the pallet to the airport.

Major Conrad and Major Osborn helped me do all this, and that afternoon at the airport I ended up eating lunch with them at their chow hall. Afterwards I felt much better and not nearly as lonely as I had felt earlier. I don't know what it was, but the two of them really managed to take the edge off of being left behind.

I also wasn't looking forward to camping out with the pallet on the flight line, but Colonel Coop was way ahead of me. He had me stage it by the field grade tents beside the commanding officer's quarters, and I took up residence in my own CP. So now I can do pretty much as I please. I can wash whenever I feel like it, sleep all day, read, and even go and watch movies with Colonel Coop in the trailer and still be able to watch over the pallet.

Things are much better then I thought they would be. Actually, living like this really ain't all that bad. RMCC is telling me they might be able to get the pallet out of here on the 30th, 3rd, or 9th. I'm hoping it's the 30th.

Today I drove back to King Abdul Aziz to get some last pictures of the place. ALD and some of the Marines who were moving into the headquarters buildings were already at work scrounging through the stuff we'd left behind for any goodies. I grabbed some water, MREs, and a roll of banding wire from out of the dump, took a last picture of my hand on the lock of the gate in front of the soccer stadium, and then headed back to the airport.

I still have to get the pallet tagged, agged, dagged, and done up properly, but that is about all I have left to do. Then once they get a mission number for me I can get the hell out of here.

29 April 1991

Spent the day reading and generally not doing much of anything. Good breakfast. Watching my friend the mouse poking around the tent. A good lunch. And waiting, like always.

The morning was pretty quiet until about 1300. The winds came then with a shot, blasting at the tent and whipping the sand up. You can't see anything now, and I am just sitting inside reading, listening to it blow outside. It kind of reminds me of being up at Lonesome Dove and of being whited out in the midst of the light sandstorms. It isn't as bad as yesterday, when the wind blew sand and dust all over the place inside and outside the tent, covering everything with a thin layer of dust and fine sand. Today it is just enough to cool the tent down by keeping fresh air moving through it.

30 April 1991

Another day past. Woke up, ran, showered, ate lunch, read for a bit, a biography Hoss gave me on Lawrence of Arabia, watched *Black Rain* with Colonel Coop, then went over to the RMCC, where I caught the end of *Grease II* and the whole of *From the Halls of Montezuma* and had dinner. Then back with Colonel Coop for *Lethal Weapon II* and *Bloodsport*. Man, am I movied out.

Chapter 6
May

1 May 1991

Tomorrow we are supposed to be going home, and I can hardly believe it. I looked at the moon and stars again tonight. It has become so quiet now since almost everybody is gone. Whole days pass with no air activity, which seems strange because it was never like this during the war. It also felt strange realizing that this was probably my last night in Saudi Arabia. In days I will be looking at the same moon and stars from halfway around the world, and I'll be with my wife again.

Today I got the pallet staged at the flightline for the custom and agricultural inspections tomorrow, picked up the messages I'm taking back for Colonel Coop and some personal gear and war trophies for Major Minton, and packed up my own stuff. I can't imagine what homecoming will be like. Will Maryanne even know I'm coming? Will there be people there to meet us? Are we even getting out of here?

I'm looking around the tent, trying to take it all in. The single bulb screwed into the socket, the tent flap closed, the Alberto VO5 shampoo bottle almost empty, the wrapping paper I'm using as a floor mat, the mouse. Someday in the future I will look back on this moment, this time, thinking back to when I was young, strong, and healthy and I had the whole world ahead of me. And I know I'll miss this because it will be a time that is long past. I'm in that future man now, just as he is in me. I see this in the faces of the old men who watch the victory parades go by, the ones who fought in World War I, World War II, Korea, and Vietnam.

Especially in the face of the man whose picture I saw in *Life*, who was watching Army Airborne troops parade past him at home. He had been in Airborne during the Normandy invasion, and to see him there in the picture fifty years later, looking like any other older man watching a parade, a bit too heavy and definitely out of shape, in contrast to the strapping young men walking past him, made me think of just how quickly it all passes. He used to be one of us and took part in one of the greatest assaults in history, but that event, which I'm sure to him seems like yesterday, is now but a memory. Just as all this will be at some point when I wake up and realize that my young life has long since passed. Can't let that happen too quickly, or without a fight — Maryanne, I'm coming home!

2 May 1991

1030

Finished with all the inspections on the pallet. Now it is being staged for loading, and I'm just waiting. It's already getting really hot today. The inside of the tent is heavy with the day's heat, and I'm beginning to sweat. Should I go for a last run or not? Probably not. If I do, I'll never stop sweating. Time to get caught up with my notes. They just cleaned the portable toilets, and that nasty smell is drifting through the camp and into my tent.

Joe Espinoza and SSgt. Herman showed up at the RMCC this morning. They were pretty pissed off because there are still fifty-four Marines down at Shaikh Isa who haven't been scheduled to get out of here. Fifty-four Marines that were stationed with MWSS-373, and almost to a man augmentees from MWSS-372. I'll bet Colonel Mitchell is tearing his hair out back home about the way some of the other squadrons have been treating his people. All the rest of MWSS-373 is already out of here. I guess the augmentees are supposed to fend for themselves.

From talking to Joe and the gunney in charge of RMCC, I have a pretty clear idea of how this happened. The gunney had scheduled them to fly out on two different planes over the course of the last week, but nobody from MWSS-373 had been in touch with the RMCC about leaving, so RMCC figured they had already been taken care of.

From what I gathered, the problem was that Warrant Officer Perry and Major Bacall never got the TPFD done up properly and couldn't give the RMCC an accurate count of the number of people MWSG-37 still had in country. So the RMCC was never really sure how many people we still had to get out of here. Maybe Richard or Major Bacall figured the squadrons could or would take care of it themselves, while the squadrons were expecting the Group to take care of it. Either way it still leaves Joe, SSgt. Herman, and fifty-four other augmentees from MWSS-372 and other organizations stranded down at Shaikh Isa.

And where are Richard and Major Bacall? Why, home, of course.

The gunney said his experiences working with us were a real pain in the ass because of problems just like this. He also told Joe and SSgt. Herman to calm down and that he would have them out of here as soon as he could, probably in not more than a day or so.

1430

Just about done packing. I'm starting to feel a headache coming on, which is normal for me whenever I'm making a big move like this. I'm trying to relax now and quit thinking about everything so it goes away. If I can keep myself from worrying about the pallet and all my gear, I'll be fine.

3 May 1991

Right now we are in a C-141 above the Atlantic Ocean, headed for MacGuire Air Force Base in New Jersey. We left Jubail Airport for Dahran at about 2230 last night, had a four- or five-hour stop over there, and then finally took off for home at 0300 this morning.

We had another stop over at Mildenhall, England. It was about 46 degrees out, rainy, green, and beautiful. The chill, the smell, it reminded me of when Rick and I visited the U.K. two years ago. I felt great, completely exhilarated, and ready to pound a few Guinnesses. But they wouldn't let us out of the terminal. So instead of the Guinness Stout and ploughman's lunch that I had been looking forward to, we got a lunch consisting of soda, chicken patty or bologna sandwiches, and candy bars.

After we waited around the terminal at Mildenhall another two hours, they rounded us all up again and we took off on the third leg of our journey. Next stop, MacGuire Air Force Base, New Jersey, USA. I can't wait.

The C-141 is basically a cargo plane that can carry a few passengers. There are about ten of us on board, not including the pilots and crew, and we are all stretched out on the troop seats doing our best to make ourselves as comfortable as possible. The plane is loud as hell, and you have to wear ear plugs while flying so you don't damage your hearing. The ear plugs muffle everything except the plane's vibration, so it is hard to talk to anybody, and the cargo is jammed in right in front of you, so it is even harder to move around. It can get cold too because the plane is not all that insulated and the heating system just isn't powerful enough to make it as comfortable as everybody would like it.

But if you dress warm, relax, and wear your ear plugs, the flight can be as enjoyable as you want it to be. Besides, nobody really cares anyway because we are going home.

My pallet is in the back, the second one from the end. There are three more pallets aboard the plane, one full of Captain Morrison's tents and H/HS-37 deuce gear, and also two vehicles. One is a white Cherokee Jeep that is going to the IMEF CG; the other is a Range Rover that is going to the IMEF staff.

Can't really see the ocean out the window because of all the clouds.

I was thinking back on the last five days I spent in Saudi, and now they don't seem like the big deal I made them out to be. They went by quickly, and everything I needed done got taken care of, no problem. For the future — don't take it all so seriously. It's easy to let stuff get to you; don't let it. Be like Colonel Coop or Colonel Caldwell and take it all in stride.

1800

I had forgotten how beautiful snow is. We are passing over Greenland now, and the fields of snow below us remind me of home.

1440, EST

I think we are over the United States now. Yee-haw! Back in the U.S. of A! What a country — don't ever forget it.

1500, PST

Final leg now, going over the great United States. I guess I can end this where I began it. In flight en route to Saudi Arabia was where it began. In flight en route to Norton Air Force Base is where it will end.

I called Colonel Staunton while we were at MacGuire, and my black-hearted soul expected the worst, that I'd arrive at Norton with nobody there to meet me and have to ride the pallet back to El Toro. That Maryanne wouldn't even know I was coming until I called her and told her I was back and that I wouldn't get home until about 0300 tomorrow morning. I was wrong. Colonel Staunton, being the man he is, really came through for me.

He has already called Maryanne, and she will be meeting me at Norton. He has also arranged for somebody from the Group to meet me at the air base to take the pallet off my hands. All I have to do is get off the plane, pass the pallet over to whoever is there, and then go home with Maryanne. On Monday I will give him the messages I have from Colonel Coop, and after that I'm free to spend some time with my wife.

I'll tell you. When he told me that, I almost cried. It's something I will always remember, him looking out for me like that, and because of it I feel that I would do anything for him from here on out. That is what a leader is. He came through for me, and for my own sake I would bust my ass to never let him down after this. I guess this is the kind of response that leadership like that brings out in a person. Now I know what they mean by looking out for your people.

It's wonderful looking out the window of the airplane at this great, big, beautiful land. I called Maryanne back at MacGuire but couldn't get through to her until just before the plane was about to leave. She sounded great and can't wait to see me. I also talked to Mom, Dad, Kerry, and Ryan, who were all happy to have me home. Mom even cried a little.

And now I'm just eagerly anticipating seeing my wife. I can imagine so many ways of how it will be. Anxiety, nerves about the long separation, but also a new awareness of just how lucky I am to be in love and loved.

I guess that is as nice a note as any on which to end this. And looking back over the past five months, I realize how lucky I was to be over there and how lucky I am to be coming back. It is easy to forget that at least eighty Americans who were over there won't be coming back. Their families won't be having any homecomings, only painful memories and the slow mending of lives that were painfully and sadly shattered by their loved ones' sacrifices. Don't ever forget them and the blood price they paid for what we so often take for granted.

Thinking back on Kevin, Hoss, Tony, Jerry, McEntire, Bose, Flynn, Scott, Hall, Hendrix, James, Pescatore, and all the rest of my crew, Zeke, Okie, Stocks, Clise, Coleman, Hart, Ali, Davidson, English, Saks, Danielson, Noonan, Gareth, Snipes, Whitaker, Major Stevenson, "Grumpy," Captain Daley, Major Osborn, Cricket, Jose, Chris, James, Rick, Dave, Marc, Dan, I realize that as James Webb said in *Fields of Fire*, they were "all part of it."

Military History

Sean Coughlin graduated from the United States Naval Academy in Annapolis, Maryland, and received his commission as a second lieutenant in the U.S. Marine Corps in May 1987. He attended the Marine Corps's Basic School in Quantico, Virginia, and then logistics school in Little Creek, Virginia. Lieutenant Coughlin was then assigned to Marine Wing Support Squadron 372 at Camp Pendleton, California, as the maintenance management officer.

In July of 1990, Saddam Hussein invaded Kuwait, and Lieutenant Coughlin deployed with Marine Wing Support Group (MWSG) 37, his parent command, to Saudi Arabia as a special staff officer. While attached to MWSG-37, he provided all essential services, including billeting and food services as well as fuel and water supplies, to the Third Marine Air Wing. Lieutenant Coughlin served in this capacity for the duration of the war and was instrumental during redeployment in making sure that MWSG-37, with all assets, got home safe and sound.

For services rendered during the conflict in Saudi Arabia, Lieutenant Coughlin received the Kuwaiti Campaign Medal with three bronze stars, an Overseas Deployment Medal, the Kuwaiti Defense Medal, and a Navy Achievement Medal. Sean Coughlin received his Master of Fine Arts Degree from the University of California in Los Angeles in the winter of 1995. Today he is a film director living in Santa Barbara, California.

Index

Index